"Struggling with post-traumatic stress disorder (PTSD) c[...] quality of life. And finding ways to move forward can be ch[...] *Behavioral Coping Skills Workbook for PTSD* synthesizes a[...] [...] and offers readers a clear path toward expanding their coping repertoire and making meaningful life changes."

>—**Susan M. Orsillo, PhD**, professor of psychology at Suffolk University, and
>coauthor of *Worry Less, Live More* and *Mindfulness- and Acceptance-Based
>Behavioral Therapies in Practice*

"For those struggling after a traumatic life experience, this book offers practical steps to identify symptoms of PTSD, along with cutting-edge cognitive behavioral strategies. Readers can then choose which symptoms are most bothersome, and systematically address each one. Importantly, the authors also include strategies that can help readers to increase positive emotions and well-being. This is a practical, reader-friendly book written by leaders in the field of trauma, emotion regulation, and management of impulsive, risky behavior. I highly recommend this book for those trying to manage their PTSD symptoms, as well as for clinicians who may be seeking a companion text in therapy."

>—**Sandra B. Morissette, PhD**, professor of clinical psychology at
>The University of Texas at San Antonio

"In this outstanding manual, Tull, Gratz, and Chapman—leading experts in the field of emotion regulation—apply their considerable knowledge and skills to helping people with PTSD. If you are struggling with the emotional aftermath of a traumatic experience, this manual will walk you through the steps of managing out-of-control emotions, facing fears, correcting distorted thinking patterns, and increasing positive feelings. I anticipate that this book will help a great many people, and will recommend it to my own patients."

>—**David Tolin, PhD**, author of *Face Your Fears*

"*The Cognitive Behavioral Coping Skills Workbook for PTSD* provides an extremely helpful, evidence-based, accessible guide to addressing the range of challenges that people with PTSD face. Tull, Gratz, and Chapman draw from their research knowledge and clinical expertise to provide a range of strategies that can help people recovering from trauma to engage more fully in their lives. By grouping strategies according to different clusters of symptoms, they've created a book that can easily be used by people who are facing different challenges. The evidence-based strategies are helpful for those in great distress, as well as for those who are struggling less, but still want some help with lingering effects of trauma."

—**Lizabeth Roemer, PhD**, professor of psychology at the University of
Massachusetts Boston, and coauthor of *Worry Less, Live More*

"This workbook represents a major step forward for improving the acquisition and retention of cognitive behavioral therapy (CBT) skills. The authors are in an exceptionally good position, as clinicians and researchers, to identify needed skills and focus upon them in the therapeutic context. This book is strongly recommended for clinicians and for the clinics in which they work. It's an important advance in the care of patients with trauma exposure and PTSD symptoms."

—**Terence M. Keane, PhD**, associate chief of staff, research and development,
VA Boston Healthcare System; director of the behavioral science division at
the National Center for PTSD; and professor of psychiatry and psychology
and assistant dean for research at Boston University School of Medicine

"I have been waiting for this book (or one like it) for many years! There are lots of self-help books out there on overcoming trauma, but none is as firmly grounded in proven therapeutic strategies as this one. The book is easy to read, and filled with examples and exercises that bring the therapy to life. The experience, expertise, and compassion of the authors shine through. Everyone who struggles with post-traumatic stress should read this book, and so should their therapists!"

—**Martin M. Antony, PhD, ABPP**, professor of psychology at Ryerson University,
Toronto, Canada, and coauthor of *The Shyness and Social Anxiety Workbook* and
The Anti-Anxiety Workbook

THE
Cognitive
Behavioral
Coping Skills
Workbook
for PTSD

Overcome Fear and Anxiety
and Reclaim Your Life

MATTHEW T. TULL, PhD
KIM L. GRATZ, PhD
ALEXANDER L. CHAPMAN, PhD, RPsych

New Harbinger Publications, Inc.

Publisher's Note

NEW HARBINGER PUBLICATIONS is a registered trademark of New Harbinger Publications, Inc.

Distributed in Canada by Raincoast Books

Copyright © 2016 by Matthew T. Tull, Kim L. Gratz, and Alexander L. Chapman
New Harbinger Publications, Inc.
5674 Shattuck Avenue
Oakland, CA 94609
www.newharbinger.com

Cover design by Amy Shoup

Acquired by Catharine Meyers

Edited by Jennifer Eastman

Library of Congress Cataloging-in-Publication Data on file

Printed in the United States of America

24   23   22

10   9   8   7   6   5

To all of my clients with PTSD—your courage, strength, and perseverance are admirable and inspirational. Thank you for sharing your stories of recovery and resilience.

—Matthew T. Tull

To all the trauma survivors I have had the honor of working with over the years. Your courage and strength are an inspiration.

—Kim L. Gratz

To all of the clients I have worked with and learned so much from.

—Alexander L. Chapman

Contents

Acknowledgments

I am grateful to so many people who have mentored, supported, and inspired me on my journey through my life and career. First, I would like to acknowledge all of the clients whom I have worked with through the years. I am deeply touched by the fact that you have been willing to share your stories with me and provide me with the opportunity to bear witness to your courage, commitment, and perseverance as you work toward building the life you want to live. I consider it an honor to be a part of your recovery process, and through your resilience and strength, I have gained invaluable knowledge about the human condition and spirit. All of you are an inspiration to me.

I would also like to express my gratitude to all the mentors I have had through the years, especially Lizabeth Roemer, Sandra Morissette, and Carl Lejuez. You each have had a unique influence on my life and career, and I am grateful for all the time and energy you have devoted and continue to devote to my professional life. I would also like to thank all of my collaborators and colleagues that I am also fortunate to call friends—Alex Chapman, Zach Rosenthal, Andres Viana, Jon Elhai, Laura Dixon, Aaron Lee, Mike Anestis, Nicole Weiss, Katie Dixon-Gordon, and Mike McDermott. You make this work fun, and I am continuously inspired by your intellect, creativity, and passion for the work that you do.

I also consider it a privilege to be able to write this book with Alex Chapman and Kim Gratz. I would have never taken on such an endeavor without their support and contribution. I am always impressed by their commitment to disseminating their knowledge. In reading their work for this book, I have learned a great deal from them, and I am excited to share this knowledge with my clients and students.

I would also like to express my gratitude to my parents, my brother, Chris, and my nieces, Abby and Holland. Your love and support is never-ending, and I appreciate the fact that you have always given me the freedom to choose my own path in life. Abby and Holland, the zest and excitement with which you approach your lives is also a reminder to me of the important things in life and living each day to its fullest. I am also appreciative of my in-laws, David and Linda Gratz, for your acceptance, love, and support. Finally, I am eternally grateful to my wife, Kim (who is also a coauthor on this book), and Daisy. Daisy, you help me stay mindful of the present moment and are always able to bring joy and peace to my life. As for Kim, I cannot put into words the impact you have had on my life. I am so appreciative that I get to share my journey through life with you. Thank you for your unconditional love, support, and patience.

—Matthew T. Tull

My work in the area of trauma began many years ago, when I had the privilege and honor to work with a number of trauma survivors. Their strength, courage, and resilience touched and inspired me, and motivated me to pursue research and clinical work in this area. I remain continually in awe of the strength, dedication, and perseverance of these survivors, and I am deeply honored to have had the opportunity to play a role in their recovery. I am also continually grateful for the ongoing relationships, personal and professional, with my coauthors—two people without whom my career would not be nearly as productive, meaningful, or enjoyable. Alex is now one of my longest-standing and most loved friends and collaborators, and I cannot imagine my career without him. Matt holds the role of both my closest collaborator and partner in life; his love, support, and exceptional culinary skills nourish and sustain me on a daily basis and make everything possible. Beyond Alex and Matt, I am extremely grateful for the friends and colleagues who provide ongoing and unconditional support, including Zach Rosenthal, Jen Cheavens, Laura Dixon, Andres Viana, Mike Anestis, and Liz Roemer. I am also thankful for the dedicated and supportive editorial staff at New Harbinger, especially Catharine Meyers, Katie Parr, and Nicola Skidmore. Finally, I am eternally grateful to my parents, Linda and Dave, for their unconditional love and support, and to Daisy for making this world a much better place and bringing profound love, joy, and peace into our lives.

—Kim L. Gratz

I acknowledge many people who have played an important role in my personal and professional life over the past several years. My past mentors and supervisors, Drs. Richard Farmer, Tony Cellucci, Tom Lynch, Clive Robins, and Marsha Linehan, have taught me so much. I greatly value our continued collaborations and friendships. I also value the support and wisdom of my good friend John Wagner through all of our adventures at the DBT Centre of Vancouver. I admire and appreciate Matt Tull—my coauthor, colleague, and friend—for his expertise and his ability to take what he knows and make it practical and useful for people struggling with PTSD. It has been a great pleasure writing with him, and I am particularly glad he was in charge of getting this book in on time! Working with my good friend Kim Gratz reminds me of the quote by Alan Watts: "This is the real secret of life—to be completely engaged with what you are doing in the here and now. And instead of calling it work, realize it is play." Working together with Kim on writing and research projects is what it should be—fun and enriching. The clients I have worked with over the years continue to inspire me with their ability to rise from incredible adversity and enrich the lives of those around them. Finally, I acknowledge the wonderful support and patience of my family, including my parents and my wonderful wife and sons.

—Alexander L. Chapman

CHAPTER 1

Understanding PTSD and Its Effect on Your Life

John was late for work. He hadn't been sleeping well lately, and last night was particularly bad. Not only did he have a hard time falling asleep, but he was also jarred out of a deep sleep several times due to nightmares. The last one occurred at four in the morning, and he decided to just get out of bed and watch television. He eventually dozed off, and when he woke up, he realized he was going to be late for work. This couldn't happen, as he had recently been struggling at work, and his supervisors were aware of his increasingly poor performance. He couldn't concentrate and found himself frequently distracted by the unpleasant memories and images that would unexpectedly pop into his head. He was also more irritable and short with his coworkers. John knew that the only way he was going to get to work on time was to take the highway. He hadn't taken the highway for over three months now. In fact, the last time he was on the highway was when he had had his motor vehicle accident. Since that time, he noticed that even the thought of getting on the highway brought up intense feelings of fear. To get anywhere now, he would take back roads or other routes that had fewer cars, even if it meant that his trip would take twice as long. However, he also began to recently notice that even being in his car would bring up some anxiety. As he pulled onto the on-ramp for the highway, John's heart rate shot up. He began to sweat. Every little sound around him made him jump. He felt extreme terror, and images of his accident flooded his mind. It was almost as if the accident were happening again. He felt like he was going to lose control. He knew that he could not make it to work on the highway, and he immediately pulled over onto the shoulder of the highway. He didn't know what to do. He felt paralyzed. He wanted to call his wife for help, but he had felt so distant and disconnected from her recently. He was also filled with shame for not being able to get over his accident, especially given that it was over three months ago. He felt helpless and hopeless. He put his head down on the steering wheel and began to cry.

John's experience is similar to those of many people with post-traumatic stress disorder (PTSD). It may even be similar to your own. As the name implies, PTSD is considered a trauma- and stressor-related disorder that occurs following the experience of a traumatic event. Many of the symptoms of PTSD, such as hyperarousal, sleep difficulties, avoidance of places that remind you of the traumatic event, and intrusive thoughts, are quite common following a traumatic event. They are your body's natural response to a life-threatening event, and many are designed to keep you safe from future danger. Hyperarousal symptoms may make you more aware of danger in your environment and allow you to react more quickly to any threat. Avoiding places or situations that remind you of the original event may keep you from experiencing a similar event. For many people, these symptoms lessen over time. For others, however, the symptoms persist and become worse.

Given this, some people have described PTSD as a disorder of recovery (Resick, Monson, and Chard 2008). That is, with PTSD, the recovery process gets stuck on high. It becomes disrupted, and as this occurs, symptoms become more severe, can lead to other unhealthy behaviors (for example, excessive drinking), and can interfere with your relationships, work, school, and physical and mental health. Fortunately, as you will learn in this book, there are steps you can take to shift the recovery process back into gear and lessen your symptoms of PTSD. You are in the driver's seat; you can take back control of your life. Before we get into what you can do to reduce your symptoms of PTSD, it is important that you have some background information on PTSD.

A Brief History of PTSD

Although there wasn't a lot of research done on PTSD prior to 1980, the disorder has always been around. Historically, symptoms of PTSD have been generally connected to the experience of combat and war. The symptoms have been described in literary works throughout the ages, even as early as the eighth century BCE in Homer's *Iliad* and *Odyssey*. Research on PTSD began to pick up following World War II. At that time, researchers and clinicians began to document the psychological distress experienced by soldiers, prisoners of war, and concentration-camp survivors long after the traumatic exposure ended. At that time, these symptoms were not referred to as *PTSD* but were described with terms such as *shell shock*, *war neurosis*, and *combat fatigue* (Keane and Barlow 2002). Then, in 1974, around the same time as clinicians were observing the high level of psychological distress being experienced by veterans of the Vietnam War, Drs. Ann Burgess and Linda Holmstrom documented similar psychological symptoms among rape survivors, calling it *rape trauma syndrome* (Burgess and Holmstrom 1974). Recognizing the personal and public health consequences of these symptoms, advocates for these two groups began working with researchers and clinicians to develop and bring awareness to the PTSD diagnosis as we know it today (Keane and Barlow 2002). The term *PTSD* became official with the publication of the third edition of the *Diagnostic and Statistical Manual of Mental Health Disorders* in 1980. Some changes have been made to the diagnosis since then, but the symptoms associated with PTSD have generally stayed the same.

The Symptoms of PTSD

To develop the symptoms of PTSD, you need to first experience a traumatic event. So, what is the difference between this kind of traumatic event and the highly stressful events that are common in everyday life? A traumatic event occurs when you are exposed to actual or threatened death, serious injury, or sexual violence. This can take the form of directly experiencing the event, witnessing the event, learning about the event (for example, hearing that a close friend or family member was raped), or being repeatedly exposed to unpleasant details of traumatic events, such as a police officer frequently hearing stories of child abuse (American Psychiatric Association 2013). As you can imagine, there are a number of events that can be considered traumatic. Because we often hear about PTSD in the context of war, there is the common misperception that PTSD is something experienced only by people in the military. This is definitely not the case. Along with combat, the events that can lead to PTSD include natural disasters, a serious accident, physical or sexual assault, and the sudden violent or accidental death of another person. With this definition in mind, identify what traumatic events you have experienced in exercise 1.1.

This exercise lists experiences often considered traumatic. Mark with an X whether the event happened to you or whether you witnessed it, learned about it, or experienced it as part of your job. You can also write down how old you were when the event or events occurred. The last row is blank, so you can write in an event if you experienced something that is not on this list.

Exercise 1.1. What Traumatic Events Have You Experienced?

Traumatic Event	Happened to Me	Witnessed It	Learned About It	Part of My Job
Natural disaster				
Fire				
Transportation accident				
Other serious accident				
Physical assault				
Assault with a weapon (for example, being shot)				
Sexual assault (including rape)				
War-zone exposure (including combat exposure)				
Held captive				
Life-threatening illness or injury				
Unexpected and sudden violent or accidental death				
Caused serious harm or death to another person				
Human suffering				
Other _____				

Following the experience of a traumatic event, a person may begin to experience a variety of PTSD symptoms. There are currently twenty possible symptoms of PTSD, and these symptoms are divided across four separate categories. An overview of these symptoms is presented in table 1.1.

Table 1.1. The Symptoms of PTSD

Intrusion Symptoms

1. Recurrent, unexpected, and intrusive memories of a traumatic event

2. Recurrent upsetting dreams or nightmares

3. Dissociation or flashbacks

4. Intense or prolonged distress that occurs following exposure to internal or external reminders of the event

5. Bodily reactions following exposure to such internal or external reminders

Avoidance Symptoms

1. Avoidance of or attempts to avoid memories, thoughts, or feelings associated with the event

2. Avoidance of or attempts to avoid people, places, conversations, situations, or things that bring up memories, thoughts, or feelings about the event

Negative Changes in Cognition and Mood Symptoms

1. Difficulties remembering an important part of the event

2. Persistent and extreme negative beliefs or expectations about yourself, others, and the world (for example, *I am a terrible person*, *No one can be trusted*, or *I will never be safe*)

3. Persistent and inaccurate thoughts about the cause or consequences of a traumatic event that lead to self-blame or the blaming of others

4. Persistent negative emotions (for example, shame, fear, anger, or guilt)

5. Loss of interest in activities that used to be meaningful

6. Feeling detached or estranged from others

7. Persistent inability to experience positive emotions, such as happiness, love, or joy

Hyperarousal Symptoms

1. Irritable behavior or angry outbursts, including acts of verbal or physical aggression

2. Reckless or self-destructive behavior (for example, risk-taking, self-injury, binge eating)

3. Hypervigilance

4. Exaggerated startle response

5. Difficulties concentrating

6. Sleep problems, such as difficulties falling asleep or staying asleep

The first category or "cluster" of symptoms is called *intrusion symptoms*; it consists of five symptoms. The first is the repeated experience of intrusive memories of the traumatic event. These memories are involuntary. That is, you aren't deliberately bringing up the memories, but instead, they occur unexpectedly or out of the blue. The second symptom is having repeated nightmares or unpleasant dreams. The nightmare may be an exact replay of the event, which is played over and over again. Alternatively, the nightmare may not be of the event itself but may contain elements that are related to the event in some way. You may also have nightmares about only one part of the event. The third intrusion symptom is a flashback or a feeling that the traumatic event is recurring. This symptom can vary in severity. Some people simply get caught up in thoughts or memories of the traumatic event (almost like daydreaming), whereas others completely lose awareness of their surroundings and the passage of time. In extreme cases, this type of response can be considered a form of dissociation (when you become detached, feel separated from, or lose touch with your emotional and physical experiences, and, in extreme cases, even reality). The fourth symptom is having strong and long-lasting emotional distress when you come into contact with some type of reminder of the event. These reminders can include things in your environment, such as hearing a loud crash or bang or seeing someone who looks like your attacker, or internal experiences, such as thoughts or feelings. The final intrusion symptom is having a strong bodily reaction (for example, increased heart rate) when you come into contact with such reminders.

The second cluster of PTSD symptoms is called *avoidance symptoms*. There are two avoidance symptoms. The first is the avoidance of upsetting memories, thoughts, or feelings about the traumatic event. The second is the avoidance of things that might bring up those thoughts, memories, and feelings, including certain people, places, conversations, activities, objects, or situations that are somehow related to the event. With this cluster of symptoms, it is recognized that it may not always be possible to avoid these reminders. Therefore, you are considered to have these symptoms if you put effort into trying to avoid a reminder of the event, regardless of how successful you are in avoiding it.

The third cluster of PTSD symptoms is labeled *negative changes in cognition and mood*. Basically, these symptoms describe changes in how you think and how you experience your emotions. There are seven symptoms in this cluster. The first is the inability to remember important parts of the traumatic event. For some people, the memory of the event may be incredibly clear. Others may not remember any of it or might remember just bits and pieces. The second symptom is long-lasting and extreme negative beliefs about yourself, other people, or the world. Following a traumatic event, it is not uncommon for certain assumptions or beliefs that many of us hold about the world, such as *People are good* or *The world is a safe place*, to be destroyed. As a result, you may develop beliefs that go to the other extreme: *People are inherently evil, I am never safe, I am permanently damaged,* or *The world is filled with constant danger.* The third symptom is an inaccurate view of the cause or result of the traumatic event that leads you to believe that you or someone else is solely to blame for it. For example, survivors of sexual assault may believe that they are to blame because they wore a certain outfit or acted in a certain way. The fourth symptom is the regular experience of unpleasant emotions, such as shame, anger, guilt, or fear. These emotions may be intense and come up frequently. The final three symptoms in this cluster are sometimes referred to as *emotional numbing symptoms*, because they describe difficulties experiencing and connecting with positive emotional experiences. These symptoms include a loss of interest in activities that used to be enjoyable or meaningful, feeling detached from others, and having a hard time experiencing positive emotions like happiness and joy.

The last cluster of PTSD symptoms is called *hyperarousal symptoms*, and there are six symptoms in this group. The first is acting in an irritable or angry manner with little or no cause. The second is engaging in reckless or self-destructive behavior, such as engaging in self-injurious behavior (for example, cutting or burning oneself), binge eating, having risky sex, or drinking excessively. The third symptom is being hypervigilant—you may feel as though some type of danger or threat is all around you, and therefore, you are constantly on guard. The fourth symptom is having an exaggerated startle response, or jumping at the slightest unexpected sound. The fifth symptom is having difficulty concentrating. PTSD symptoms can be very distracting. If thoughts or memories are flooding your mind, it is going to be difficult to focus your attention on a task at hand. High levels of anxiety can also interfere with concentration. The final symptom is having problems sleeping, whether it is falling asleep, staying asleep, or being restless when you sleep. Sleeping problems may be due to nightmares or simply the high levels of anxiety that go along with PTSD.

Being Diagnosed with PTSD

There are twenty symptoms of PTSD, but you do not need to experience all of them to be diagnosed with PTSD. You need to experience at least one symptom from the intrusion cluster, one from the avoidance cluster, two from the negative changes in cognition and mood cluster, and two from the hyperarousal cluster. In addition, you have to have experienced these symptoms for at least one month following a traumatic event, and they must cause a high level of distress and problems in different areas of your life. You may wonder why you have to have the symptoms for at least a month. Remember that we said earlier that PTSD can be viewed as a disorder of the recovery process? Many of these symptoms are commonplace following a traumatic event, but they soon begin to fade on their own as the person begins to recover from the event. If they persist for more than a month, however, it can be a sign that the recovery process isn't working the way it normally does.

Exercise 1.2 has a list of the twenty PTSD symptoms. Mark all that you have experienced in the past month.

Exercise 1.2. What PTSD Symptoms Have You Experienced in the Past Month?

_____	1.	Recurrent, unexpected, and intrusive memories of a traumatic event
_____	2.	Recurrent upsetting dreams or nightmares that are associated with the event
_____	3.	Dissociation or flashbacks
_____	4.	Intense or prolonged distress that occurs following exposure to internal or external reminders of the event
_____	5.	Bodily reactions following exposure to such internal or external reminders
_____	6.	Avoidance of or attempts to avoid memories, thoughts, or feelings associated with the event
_____	7.	Avoidance of or attempts to avoid people, places, conversations, situations, or things that bring up memories, thoughts, or feelings about the event
_____	8.	Difficulties remembering an important part of the event
_____	9.	Persistent and extreme negative beliefs or expectations about yourself, others, and the world
_____	10.	Persistent and inaccurate thoughts about the cause or consequences of a traumatic event that lead to self-blame or the blaming of others
_____	11.	Persistent negative emotions
_____	12.	Loss of interest in activities that used to be meaningful
_____	13.	Feeling detached or estranged from others
_____	14.	Persistent inability to experience positive emotions
_____	15.	Irritable behavior or anger outbursts
_____	16.	Reckless or self-destructive behavior
_____	17.	Hypervigilance
_____	18.	Exaggerated startle response
_____	19.	Difficulties concentrating
_____	20.	Sleep problems

In addition to these symptoms, PTSD can lead to other physical and mental health problems, though they are not considered part of the diagnosis. People with PTSD are at higher risk to develop heart disease, obesity, gastrointestinal problems, respiratory problems, pain, and other physical health problems (Koenen and Galea 2015). This is likely due to the toll that chronic stress takes on the body, but another contributing factor is the fact that people with PTSD are more likely to engage in behaviors that are damaging to their health, such as drinking and smoking (Beckham 1999; McFarlane 1998). In addition, people with PTSD are more likely to have other mental health disorders, such as anxiety disorders, major depression, eating disorders, and substance-use disorders (Kessler et al. 1995). Finally, PTSD can lead to a number of self-destructive behaviors, such as binge eating, self-injury, and even suicide (Tull, Weiss, and McDermott 2016).

Now, it is possible that you are someone who isn't experiencing at least six symptoms of PTSD, as required for a clinical diagnosis. Or you may be someone who experiences six symptoms, but they are in only three of the symptom clusters. Does this mean you don't have PTSD? If these symptoms have persisted for over a month, are causing a high level of emotional distress, and interfere with your living your life, then those symptoms require attention. People who fall into this category are considered to have *subthreshold PTSD*. Studies have found that these people can experience problems similar to those seen among people with full-blown PTSD, such as mental health disorders, problems at work or socially, and thoughts of suicide (Marshall et al. 2001; Zlotnick, Franklin, and Zimmerman 2002).

Who Gets PTSD?

Traumatic events are common; almost 90 percent of people will be directly exposed to, witness, or learn about a traumatic event at some point in their lifetime (Breslau and Kessler 2001). However, only a small proportion (around 7 percent) will eventually develop PTSD (Kessler et al. 2005). You may be wondering what determines whether someone develops PTSD. That's a great question, but unfortunately, there isn't a clear answer. A number of studies have been conducted that tried to determine who may be at greater risk for developing PTSD, and although researchers haven't found a definitive answer, they have identified a number of factors that seem to increase a person's vulnerability for PTSD. There are a lot of studies out there, so we are only going to go through a couple of these factors.

The type of traumatic event you experienced can have an impact on whether you develop PTSD. Certain types of traumatic events have been found to be more likely to lead to PTSD than others. For example, experiences of a rape, molestation as a child, physical assault, or combat have all been found to be more likely to lead to PTSD than things like car accidents and natural disasters. In fact, rape has been found to be associated with some of the highest rates (even higher than combat exposure), which may explain why PTSD seems to occur more often in women (Kessler et al. 1995). People who have experienced more severe traumatic events, as well as multiple traumatic or stressful events, are also more likely to develop PTSD. People who are lower in socioeconomic status also seem to be at greater risk, although it is not exactly clear why this is the case (Brewin, Andrews, and Valentine 2000). It is possible that people with a lower income are more likely to live in places where there is a greater risk for being exposed to traumatic events (for example, due to higher crime rates) and in places where there are fewer mental health resources. Indeed, after the experience of a traumatic event, the availability of social support and healthy coping skills is key to reducing the risk of developing PTSD, and so when resources that can help foster support and coping are not available, PTSD may be more likely to occur (Agaibi and Wilson 2005). That is why, even if you don't have PTSD, learning healthy coping skills (such as the ones presented in this book) can help you after the experience of a traumatic event.

Why Does PTSD Develop?

When a traumatic event occurs, people experience strong emotions, such as fear, sadness, anger, and horror. Whether you are aware of it or not, aspects of your environment—both external (sounds, smells, objects, and people) and internal (for example, bodily sensations and thoughts)—that are present at the time of a traumatic event become associated with those emotions through a process called *classical conditioning*. Classical conditioning is one way in which learning occurs. Have you ever heard of Pavlov's dogs? In the 1890s, a Russian psychologist named Ivan Pavlov was doing research on salivation in dogs when eating. He noticed that the dogs he was studying began to salivate whenever he entered the room, even before he gave them their food. This led him to run some studies in which he paired the ringing of a bell with the presentation of food to the dogs. Over time, he observed that the bell alone was enough to cause the dogs to salivate, even when the food was no longer provided. That is, the bell became a signal that the food was going to be delivered.

A similar process occurs when a person experiences a traumatic event. The emotion of fear (or any other emotion that occurs) becomes associated or connected with other things or experiences that are present at the time of the traumatic event. These things then have the potential to bring up the fear and memories of the traumatic event at any time. For example, a woman is sexually assaulted, and during the sexual assault, the strong smell of her perpetrator's cologne becomes fixed in her memory. In her mind, the smell of that cologne became connected with the fear, helplessness, and horror that she felt during the sexual assault, and now, whenever she smells something similar to that cologne, it activates unpleasant memories and emotions, even if she knows that she is in no actual danger of being assaulted. Similarly, in the case of John, from the beginning of the chapter, certain situations (the highway and his car) and experiences (loud noises) became associated with his traumatic event, a motor vehicle accident. Therefore, whenever he encounters these situations or experiences, he begins to have strong feelings of fear.

As people repeatedly experience these unpleasant emotions and thoughts, they are naturally motivated to avoid the things that trigger them. For example, John goes out of his way not to drive on highways. A veteran with PTSD from combat may stay away from fireworks displays and other situations where there are likely to be loud noises. This makes sense, as we are naturally motivated to avoid things that cause us pain, both physical and emotional. In fact, this is part of the body's natural defense mechanism, the fight-flight-or-freeze response—basically your internal alarm system. When you are in danger or sense danger, this response is activated, and it prepares you to fight, flight, or freeze as a way of protecting yourself. It is automatic—it occurs without your putting any thought into it. Think about a recent time when you were very afraid of something. You may have noticed that your muscles became tense, you began to sweat, your attention narrowed, and your heart began to beat faster. All of these experiences were due to your body's alarm system going off; they were preparing you to act in some way. Although this response is helpful, it also has some downsides, especially when PTSD is concerned. The system isn't always good at determining whether a threat is real or imagined. A combat veteran may have his fight-flight-or-freeze response activated when he watches a movie that has loud explosions in it. In actuality, the veteran is in no real danger, but his body's alarm system is telling him that he is in danger and should avoid the situation.

This avoidance works well in bringing down distress in the short term, but it can eventually cause PTSD symptoms to worsen, because it is another way in which learning occurs, called *operant conditioning*. When we engage in a certain behavior (such as avoiding movies that have explosions) and have some kind of desired outcome (in this case, lower distress), we will be more likely to engage in that behavior again. Over time, this behavior can become habitual, occurring with limited awareness on our part. Repeated avoidance also sends the message that there is something real to fear. In addition, as people experience fear in new situations and begin to avoid those situations as well, their body's alarm system becomes more and more sensitive. A growing number of things will begin to trigger PTSD symptoms (we will talk more about triggers in chapter 2 and help you identify your own triggers). Eventually, people may begin to feel that they are never safe. You can think of avoidance as the fuel for PTSD symptoms. Although it seems like avoidance is keeping you safe in the short term, this sense of safety is short lived, and in the long term, it can interfere with the processing of emotions associated with the traumatic event you experienced and slow your recovery (Foa and Kozak 1986; Litz and Roemer 1996).

Other models of PTSD talk about the ways in which a traumatic event negatively impacts our beliefs about ourselves and the world. As we mentioned previously, everyone holds certain assumptions or beliefs about the world, such as *Bad things don't happen to good people, The world is just and fair*, and *I am in control of my life and what happens to me*. These beliefs guide a lot of our behavior and how we view ourselves throughout our life. When a traumatic event occurs, however, extreme information is obtained that provides a tremendous amount of evidence against these beliefs. By their very nature, traumatic events force people to confront the worst things that can happen to a person. And afterward, the world is a very different place. Therefore, after a traumatic event, there is a need to reconcile this new information with previously held beliefs. Basically, you need to make sense of what happened. Sometimes, however, people's attempts to make it make sense can lead them down a path that isn't so useful for recovery. You may blame yourself for what happened. You may start to think, *Bad things don't happen to good people, so I must have been punished for doing something bad*. Or, you may go to the other extreme, thinking, *The world is never a safe place, even for good people like me*. These new beliefs are naturally going to bring up unpleasant emotions, such as shame, guilt, and anxiety, and they will lead you to avoid certain situations, which will give fuel to your PTSD symptoms (Resick, Monson, and Chard 2008).

How Is PTSD Treated?

PTSD can have a major negative impact on your life; however, there is hope. Fortunately, psychological treatments for PTSD have been developed, and there is a good amount of evidence that these treatments can help people recover from PTSD. There are two gold-standard psychological treatments for PTSD—*prolonged exposure* and *cognitive processing therapy*. We are going to focus on these two treatments, as they currently have the most research backing them up.

In prolonged exposure (Foa, Hembree, and Rothbaum 2007), the ultimate goal is to help you process the emotions connected to the experience of a traumatic event. This is done by having you come into contact with thoughts, situations, objects, and places that you associate with your traumatic event and that bring up fear. Exposure can take the form of *imaginal exposure* or *in vivo exposure*. Imaginal exposure involves imagining all of the things that happened during a traumatic event. During an imaginal exposure exercise, you may be asked to describe what you experienced with your five senses, the thoughts you had, the emotions you experienced, and what bodily sensations occurred. In vivo exposure involves confronting the actual objects, people, places, or situations that you fear. For example, if John decided to receive prolonged exposure for his PTSD stemming from a motor vehicle accident, he may be asked to look at pictures of car accidents, listen to loud sounds, and, eventually, drive on the highway. These exposure exercises are all done in a controlled and structured manner. In chapter 5 we will talk more about the different types of exposure and how they can be used to alleviate your PTSD symptoms.

You may be thinking that this sounds like a scary treatment and wonder how it could possibly help reduce PTSD symptoms. Well, remember that we said that avoidance is what fuels PTSD symptoms? During exposure exercises, you are asked to sit with the fear and not avoid it. By confronting the things that you fear, you eventually build up your tolerance for fear and learn that you are not truly in danger. Your body may be sounding the alarm, but it is a false alarm. The traumatic event is not recurring. Over time, your body's alarm system will become less sensitive and less likely to be activated when you come into contact with reminders of a traumatic event.

Cognitive processing therapy (Resick, Monson, and Chard 2008) is another psychological treatment that has been found to be successful in reducing the symptoms of PTSD. It also helps reduce avoidance behavior, but it tackles it by using different methods than prolonged exposure. Cognitive processing therapy focuses its attention on how you interpret your traumatic event, as well as on the beliefs about yourself and the world that developed after your traumatic event. Remember that we said that one theory on how PTSD develops focuses on the way in which a traumatic event leads to negative beliefs about yourself and the world. These beliefs lead to a number of unpleasant emotions, hopelessness, self-blame, helplessness, and avoidance behavior. Cognitive processing therapy refers to these beliefs as *stuck points*, because they keep you stuck, interfering with your recovery from a traumatic event.

Cognitive processing therapy targets these stuck points. This treatment helps you identify these patterns of unhealthy thinking and assists you in looking at your experience from a more flexible, accurate, and compassionate perspective. In doing so, unpleasant emotions and thoughts are reduced, leading to less avoidance and other unhealthy behavior. Chapter 4 in this book will take you through some of cognitive processing therapy's strategies for identifying and addressing stuck points. Exposure is also part of cognitive processing therapy, but it looks different than what occurs in prolonged exposure. In cognitive processing therapy, you are asked to write about your traumatic event. You are then asked to read your description of the traumatic event to your therapist in session. Although this exercise helps break down avoidance using exposure, as you recount the details of the event, the primary goal is to help you identify and begin to address stuck points.

Ready to Start on the Road to Recovery?

We hope that after reading this chapter, you have a better understanding of the symptoms of PTSD and why they develop. We also would like to think that you have a greater sense of hope about recovering from your PTSD. A tremendous amount of research has been done on PTSD, and there are effective treatments available, with more being developed and studied all the time. In fact, it is because there are so many treatments supported by research that we were able to develop this book.

Instead of taking you through a single treatment approach, we have pulled together a variety of skills from a number of different treatments for PTSD and related conditions that will help address specific symptoms of PTSD that you may be struggling with. Each chapter is focused on a set of PTSD-related symptoms, such as intrusive thoughts, problems managing emotions, nightmares, impulsive behaviors, sleep problems, and difficulties experiencing positive emotions. Within these chapters, we then take you through a number of different skills that can help you better manage these experiences. All of the skills come from treatments that are supported by research, such as prolonged exposure for PTSD (Foa, Hembree, and Rothbaum 2007), cognitive processing therapy for PTSD (Resick, Monson, and Chard 2008), dialectical behavior therapy (Linehan 1993a), imagery rehearsal therapy for nightmares (Krakow and Zadra 2010), behavioral activation (Lejuez et al. 2011), and acceptance and commitment therapy (Hayes, Strosahl, and Wilson 2011).

We decided to take this approach because PTSD can look very different from one person to the next. Not everyone with PTSD struggles with the same symptoms. Therefore, you can go through this book and pick and choose the skills that you think are going to work best for you. That said, we think that before you move on to any of the skills that are focused on specific PTSD symptoms, we think that it will be useful for you to learn some basic skills for managing triggers for PTSD symptoms and anxiety. Therefore, we would advise that you go through chapters 2 and 3 first before going on to any of the later chapters. The skills presented in these chapters will provide you with a nice foundation that you can build on later. So, with that said, the first step in addressing your PTSD symptoms is figuring out the specific symptoms you need to focus on. This process begins in the next chapter. Let's get started.

CHAPTER 2

Increasing Awareness of Your PTSD Symptoms and Their Cues

Now that you have some basic information on PTSD, let's start the process of helping you cope with your symptoms. This chapter is focused on increasing your awareness of your PTSD symptoms and the types of things that cue or trigger those symptoms. You may be thinking, *I am already too aware of my symptoms. Why would I want to bring more awareness to them?* This makes a lot of sense. Symptoms of PTSD can be intense and frequent, making it hard to *not* be aware of them. However, as apparent as PTSD symptoms are when they occur, it is important to understand which symptoms you struggle with most, which symptoms tend to occur most often, and what types of situations or things bring about your symptoms. Without this increased awareness, PTSD symptoms may feel as though they sometimes come out of the blue. As this occurs more and more, the symptoms may feel unpredictable and out of control, which can lead to even more anxiety.

By improving your awareness of your symptoms and their cues, they may seem more predictable. You will also likely have a better idea of how to cope with your symptoms. For example, if you know that you are experiencing a symptom more strongly than you normally do, this could tell you that you are isolating more or not taking care of yourself as much as you need to. This information can then direct you to take some healthy corrective steps. Likewise, by knowing what triggers a symptom, you can plan ahead to ensure that you aren't blindsided by it. So, let's start by helping you gain a better awareness of your PTSD symptoms and how you experience them.

How Do You Experience Your PTSD Symptoms?

As we discussed in the previous chapter, there are four clusters of PTSD symptoms (intrusion, avoidance, negative changes in cognition and mood, and hyperarousal). The first set of symptoms that we are going to focus on is the intrusion symptoms. As a reminder, this cluster of symptoms includes thoughts, memories, nightmares, and feelings of distress that repeatedly enter into your awareness, often without warning.

Below, in exercise 2.1, each intrusion symptom is listed. Think about the past month. Now ask yourself, how often have you experienced that symptom? Check off the best answer in the column titled "Frequency." Finally, we want to get an idea of how intense or severe that symptom is when it is experienced. So, in the final column, labeled "Severity," rate how severe the symptom generally is on a scale from 0 to 10. A severity rating of 0 would mean that the symptom is not distressing to you, isn't intense, doesn't last long, and really doesn't interfere with your life. A rating of 10 would mean that the symptom causes extreme distress, is very intense, lasts a long time, and greatly interferes with your life.

As you go through this exercise, you may notice that it isn't easy to always come up with an answer. Some weeks in the past month may have been better than others. That's okay. Just try to give your best response, one that reflects the average or general frequency and severity of each symptom over the past month.

Exercise 2.1. Intrusion Symptoms

Symptoms	Frequency	Severity (0–10)
Recurrent, unexpected, and intrusive memories of a traumatic event	_____ Never _____ Once or twice _____ Once or twice a week _____ 3+ times a week _____ Almost every day	
Recurrent upsetting dreams or nightmares	_____ Never _____ Once or twice _____ Once or twice a week _____ 3+ times a week _____ Almost every day	
Dissociation or flashbacks	_____ Never _____ Once or twice _____ Once or twice a week _____ 3+ times a week _____ Almost every day	
Intense or prolonged distress that occurs following exposure to internal or external reminders of a traumatic event	_____ Never _____ Once or twice _____ Once or twice a week _____ 3+ times a week _____ Almost every day	
Bodily reactions following exposure to those internal or external reminders	_____ Never _____ Once or twice _____ Once or twice a week _____ 3+ times a week _____ Almost every day	

Now, let's move to the cluster of avoidance symptoms. As the name implies, these symptoms all refer to attempts you may make to try to avoid or escape your PTSD symptoms.

Exercise 2.2. Avoidance Symptoms

Symptoms	Frequency	Severity (0–10)
Avoidance of or attempts to avoid memories, thoughts, or feelings associated with a traumatic event	_____ Never _____ Once or twice _____ Once or twice a week _____ 3+ times a week _____ Almost every day	
Avoidance of or attempts to avoid people, places, conversations, situations, or things that bring up memories, thoughts, or feelings about a traumatic event	_____ Never _____ Once or twice _____ Once or twice a week _____ 3+ times a week _____ Almost every day	

The next cluster of symptoms refers to changes in thoughts and mood that occurred after you experienced a traumatic event.

Exercise 2.3. Negative Changes in Thoughts and Mood

Symptoms	Frequency	Severity (0–10)
Difficulties remembering an important part of a traumatic event	_____ Never _____ Once or twice _____ Once or twice a week _____ 3+ times a week _____ Almost every day	
Persistent and extreme negative beliefs or expectations about yourself, others, and the world (for example, *I am a terrible person, No one can be trusted, I will never be safe*)	_____ Never _____ Once or twice _____ Once or twice a week _____ 3+ times a week _____ Almost every day	
Persistent and inaccurate thoughts about the cause or consequences of a traumatic event that lead to self-blame or the blaming of others	_____ Never _____ Once or twice _____ Once or twice a week _____ 3+ times a week _____ Almost every day	
Persistent negative emotions (for example, shame, fear, anger, or guilt)	_____ Never _____ Once or twice _____ Once or twice a week _____ 3+ times a week _____ Almost every day	
Loss of interest in activities that used to be meaningful	_____ Never _____ Once or twice _____ Once or twice a week _____ 3+ times a week _____ Almost every day	

Symptoms	Frequency	Severity (0–10)
Feeling detached or estranged from others	_____ Never _____ Once or twice _____ Once or twice a week _____ 3+ times a week _____ Almost every day	
Persistent inability to experience positive emotions (such as happiness, love, or joy)	_____ Never _____ Once or twice _____ Once or twice a week _____ 3+ times a week _____ Almost every day	

The final cluster emphasizes symptoms of hyperarousal and reactivity. This cluster also includes sleep problems, difficulties concentrating, and engaging in risky or self-destructive behavior, such as self-injury.

Exercise 2.4. Hyperarousal Symptoms

Symptoms	Frequency	Severity (0–10)
Irritable behavior or angry outbursts, including acts of verbal or physical aggression	_____ Never _____ Once or twice _____ Once or twice a week _____ 3+ times a week _____ Almost every day	

Symptoms	Frequency	Severity (0–10)
Reckless or self-destructive behavior (for example, risk-taking, self-injury, binge eating)	_____ Never _____ Once or twice _____ Once or twice a week _____ 3+ times a week _____ Almost every day	
Hypervigilance	_____ Never _____ Once or twice _____ Once or twice a week _____ 3+ times a week _____ Almost every day	
Exaggerated startle response	_____ Never _____ Once or twice _____ Once or twice a week _____ 3+ times a week _____ Almost every day	
Difficulties concentrating	_____ Never _____ Once or twice _____ Once or twice a week _____ 3+ times a week _____ Almost every day	
Sleep problems, such as difficulties falling asleep or staying asleep	_____ Never _____ Once or twice _____ Once or twice a week _____ 3+ times a week _____ Almost every day	

Going through these exercises may not have been easy, but it is a major step forward in addressing your PTSD symptoms. Sometimes bringing awareness to your symptoms can make them feel a little more intense. But by acknowledging and focusing on them, you are already starting the process of breaking down avoidance of these symptoms. In addition, you now should have a better idea of which symptoms are having the greatest impact on you. This information tells you what you may need to focus on first, and it can direct you toward certain chapters in this book that deal with those particular symptoms.

As you go through your recovery from PTSD, it can be a good idea to revisit this exercise and track your symptoms. Print copies of these tables (available for download at http://www .newharbinger.com/32240) and evaluate how frequent and severe your symptoms have been every two to four weeks. If you notice that some symptoms are improving, this is an excellent sign and can give you motivation to keep moving forward in implementing and learning new skills for addressing your PTSD symptoms. If you notice that some symptoms have stayed the same or become worse, this gives you important information that you need to take additional steps to address them.

Identifying Your PTSD Symptom Triggers

Your cues, or triggers, are anything that activates or brings on a PTSD symptom. Triggers can be external or internal (outside or inside you). Generally, triggers begin as things that are directly connected to your traumatic event. For example, if you were in a severe motor vehicle accident, you may notice that intrusive memories of the accident are brought on by being on the highway where the accident occurred, being in a car going at a high speed, or smelling burnt rubber. Because these things bring up PTSD symptoms, people generally try to avoid places or activities where triggers are likely. Or, if one of these triggers appears unexpectedly, they immediately get out of the situation. While this makes sense in the short term (it is natural to want to get away from painful experiences), in the long term, as this avoidance continues, things that are not as directly connected to the traumatic event may become triggers. For example, PTSD symptoms might eventually be triggered just by being in a car, even if it is not moving; smelling tar being used in road construction; seeing a picture of a highway; or traveling at a high speed in any other type of situation (for example, on a carnival ride). Basically, anything can eventually trigger a PTSD symptom.

PTSD symptoms can also be brought on by experiences inside us. For example, if your heart was racing during a traumatic event, this bodily sensation may bring up thoughts or feelings associated with that event. If you experienced pain in a certain part of your body during a traumatic event, the experience of a similar pain in that part of your body may trigger memories.

Other internal triggers may include muscle tension, shortness of breath, or feeling vulnerable, lonely, or out of control.

Both internal and external triggers can be difficult to avoid. For example, you may notice that every year, when you approach the anniversary of your traumatic event, you start to experience an increase in your PTSD symptoms. There is no way to avoid the passage of time, and even if there were, avoidance really isn't the best long-term solution for dealing with your symptoms. We will talk more about how to prevent avoidance in chapter 5, when we talk about exposure. For now, the best way to manage your triggers is to become more aware of what they are, so you can be better prepared to cope with them when they occur. There are also steps that you can take to lessen their impact on your symptoms. Exercise 2.5, below, will help you begin to increase your awareness of your triggers.

With this exercise, we want you to keep track of situations (both internal and external) that bring about your PTSD symptoms. If you notice a symptom occurring, write in the first column the date and time when it occurred. As you work through this exercise, you may notice that you are more vulnerable to symptoms at certain times of the day or certain days of the week.

In the next column, labeled "Situation," write down what type of situation you were in. Were you watching a television show? Did you experience a certain physical sensation? Did you smell something? Be as specific as possible. You want to make sure you are clear about what specifically triggered a symptom.

The next three columns are for determining what exactly you experienced when these symptoms were triggered. In the first column, labeled "Thoughts," write down what types of thoughts came up for you. Did you have vivid memories of your traumatic event? Did you worry about the event occurring again? In the next column, labeled "Emotions," write down any emotion that you felt. Did you experience fear, guilt, sadness, or anger? Maybe you experienced multiple emotions. If you are having a hard time identifying the specific emotion that you experienced, that's okay. Just write down whatever you can connect with. In the next column, "Bodily Sensations," write down whatever feelings you had in your body. Did you notice increased heart rate, sweating, muscle tension, pain, or trembling?

The final column is labeled "Response." In this column, we want you to write down what you did in response to being confronted with your PTSD symptoms after a trigger. Did you avoid? Did you lash out at someone? Did you cry? Did you seek out social support? This is an important column, because it can help you identify the unhealthy and healthy coping strategies that you are currently using to manage your PTSD triggers and symptoms.

Exercise 2.5. Identifying Your PTSD Triggers

Date and Time	Situation	Thoughts	Emotions	Bodily Sensations	Response

Coping with Triggers

As we mentioned previously, it is hard to avoid triggers. Triggers for PTSD symptoms can be all around us and sometimes even inside of us. Given this, it is important that you learn coping strategies that can help limit the impact of a trigger on your symptoms. The first strategy is mindfulness of your external environment. *Mindfulness* refers to a particular form of attention. It involves approaching your experience of the present moment nonjudgmentally, without evaluating it any way. In other words, mindful attention is about being aware of the present moment as it is, as opposed to what our mind tells us it is. In this way, mindfulness can be a particularly useful coping strategy for managing triggers. Triggers and the anxiety that follows can narrow your attention, making it difficult to disengage attention from a trigger or the thoughts and emotions that come up as a result of a trigger. Exercise 2.6 is designed to expand your awareness to everything that is going on around you and to prevent you from focusing just on the trigger or symptoms.

Exercise 2.6. Mindfulness of Your External Environment

1. Spend a minute or two just scanning your environment. Instead of focusing your attention on a trigger or your symptoms, expand your awareness to notice everything that is going on around you. Notice and describe out loud what you see around you. List the different things that you see, such as a tree, a bird, or a house. Do your best to describe in vivid detail every object in your awareness. Pretend that you are trying to describe your environment to someone on the phone. What colors do you see? How large or small are objects in your environment? Are objects moving or standing still? Where are they located in your field of vision?

2. Now bring your awareness to what you hear. If you feel comfortable closing your eyes, do so. Notice all the sounds around you. Sounds in front of you, behind you, to the side of you, or below you. Try to notice even subtle sounds or brief moments of silence. You may also want to try to describe the details of all of the sounds that you hear.

3. If relevant, you can also bring awareness to what you smell. If you are in a restaurant, try to notice all the different smells in the air. Are the smells constant or fleeting? How strong are they? Describe what smells you are experiencing.

4. Now bring your awareness to what you feel on the surface of your body. If you are outside, notice the air against your skin. Notice what your clothes feel like against your body. If you are standing, notice what it feels like to have your feet firmly planted on the ground.

5. If your eyes are closed, open them and bring awareness to what you see, hear, smell, and feel. Allow yourself to be receptive to all experiences as they arise, whenever they arise. If you notice that your attention becomes focused on your PTSD symptoms or a trigger, that's okay. Simply acknowledge that your attention went back to the symptoms or trigger, and then gently bring your awareness back to your entire external environment.

This is a great skill to have in your back pocket, because it is one that you can use at any point in time, no matter where you are. If you encounter a trigger, breathe and move through your five senses. Observe and describe what you see, hear, smell, taste, and feel. You can also use the acronym STOP—*Stop, Take a breath, Observe what's going on around you,* and *Proceed* (i.e., move forward with what you were doing before the trigger caught your attention). As you use this exercise (as well as any other mindfulness exercise in this book), remember that mindfulness is a skill that requires practice. When you first use this skill, you may notice that the trigger keeps grabbing your attention. That's okay. It's going to happen. Notice that and then bring your attention back to your breath and then your external environment. The more you can redirect your attention, the more you will weaken a trigger's grip over you. Mindfulness is about being distracted one hundred times and bringing your attention back to the present moment 101 times.

The second coping strategy related to mindfulness of your external environment is *grounding*. The mindfulness practiced in exercise 2.6 is a kind of grounding, in that being mindful of your external environment can help ground you—keep you in the present moment—more generally, but there are also more specialized grounding activities that connect you with the present moment quickly and completely. This makes grounding a particularly helpful strategy for triggers that bring about flashbacks or dissociation, which can quickly take us out of the present moment. Grounding jolts you back into reality. Grounding exercises come in many forms. Experiment with the activities listed in exercise 2.7. In the blank lines, list some additional grounding exercises that you think may be helpful for you. In coming up with your own list, try to think about grounding exercises that you can use in different situations and at different times. For example, there may be some times when it will be possible for you to take a cold shower to ground yourself. However, this strategy isn't going to work if you are in a meeting at work. The more options you have available, the better off you will be in reducing the impact of a PTSD trigger.

Exercise 2.7. Grounding

If you notice that you are losing touch with the present moment, try one of these activities to snap you back into reality.

- Hold onto an ice cube

- Smell something with a strong odor, such as peppermint

- Listen to music

- Grab ahold of the armrest of your chair

- Bite into a lemon or eat a strong mint

- Take a cold shower or splash cold water on your face

- Touch something rough or with a lot of texture

- _____

- _____

- _____

- _____

- _____

- _____

The final coping strategy we are going to discuss is *distraction*. Distraction is designed to pull your attention away from a trigger. Distraction can be helpful for external triggers, but it may be particularly helpful for internal triggers, such as intense thoughts, emotions, or bodily sensations. When coming up with a distraction activity, you want to choose something that is interesting or stimulating. You want the distraction activity to be something that you can really get into and enjoy. One thing to keep in mind when using distraction is that distraction is designed to be a temporary activity. You want to use distraction to bring your attention away from a trigger only until that trigger has reduced in intensity and is easier to sit with. You do not want to use distraction as a form of avoidance, as this will only make that trigger stronger.

As with grounding exercises, some distraction strategies work better in some situations than others. Therefore, try to also come up with your own distraction strategies, and in doing so, come up with activities that you can do at different times and places.

Exercise 2.8. Using Distraction to Manage Triggers

When you notice a strong trigger, use distraction to temporarily bring your attention elsewhere. You may try one of the following activities:

- Do puzzles or crosswords

- Play a game on your phone

- Do some form of physical exercise (as long as the trigger you are trying to cope with is increased arousal)

- Talk to a friend about something unrelated to your PTSD

- Go window-shopping

- Read an engaging book or magazine article

- Listen to a song that you like

- Do arts and crafts

- Look at pictures of kittens

- Eat a meal or something that you enjoy

- Take a warm, soothing bath

- Look at pictures of places you have been or places you would like to go

- Drink a cup of soothing tea

- Pet or cuddle with a dog or a cat

- Count backward from one thousand by sevens

- _____

- _____

- _____

- _____

- _____

- _____

Mindfulness, grounding, and distraction can all be useful strategies for managing triggers. However, keep in mind that this is not an exhaustive list. Sometimes just basic problem solving can be a useful way of managing triggers. For example, let's say that you want to go to the movies, as this would be a great way of getting out of the house and doing something you enjoy. However, you are also struggling with hyperarousal symptoms, and loud noises tend to activate these symptoms. To deal with this dilemma, you could make the choice to see a comedy or romance film instead of an action movie with a lot of explosions, car crashes, and gunshots. You could also plan ahead and identify some coping strategies you could use if your hyperarousal symptoms occur during the movie. In this situation, knowledge of your triggers would allow you to plan ahead to cope with triggers so that you could engage in an activity that is important to you. You may also find, as you work through the rest of the book, that some of the strategies mentioned in later chapters, including emotion regulation skills and exposure, will be helpful for managing triggers. The most important thing is that you identify healthy coping strategies that are going to work best for your individual triggers and that are available to you in a number of different situations. This will give you some flexibility with regard to what coping strategies can be used, and it will give you options, in case your first coping strategy does not work so well.

Moving Forward

Congratulations on making it through the first chapter in this workbook focused on teaching you skills to manage your PTSD symptoms. In this chapter, you gained an improved awareness of your symptoms and your triggers for these symptoms. You also learned a few coping strategies for managing your triggers. By increasing your awareness of your symptoms and their triggers, the symptoms may feel more predictable and under your control. By knowing when your symptoms are more likely to come up, you can take steps to make sure you are prepared to cope with them.

PTSD symptoms and triggers can change. Therefore, as you go through this workbook, revisit this chapter periodically to see if you have noticed any change in your symptoms or triggers. In doing so, you can also get a better sense of the progress that you have made.

CHAPTER 3

Basic Strategies for Coping with Anxiety

Until 2013, PTSD was considered an anxiety disorder (American Psychiatric Association 2000). Although it is now classified as a trauma-related disorder (American Psychiatric Association 2013), PTSD is still thought of as mainly a disorder of anxiety. At the core of PTSD is the experience of severe and frequent anxiety. Although people with PTSD struggle with all kinds of intense emotions, including anger, shame, and sadness, anxiety is the most common and accounts for many of the symptoms of this disorder. The good news is that there are a number of simple strategies for managing anxiety that can be helpful for people with PTSD. Indeed, most of the treatments for PTSD that have been found to be useful focus initially on teaching clients some basic skills for managing their anxiety.

As a group, these skills are helpful for several reasons. First, they are simple. Now, this doesn't necessarily make them easy to do; any new skill can be difficult to use and master. However, the skills in this chapter have the benefit of being relatively basic and straightforward—an excellent place to start when beginning to learn new skills. Second, these skills can be used almost anywhere and at any time. Some of the skills we'll teach you later in this book require a bit more time, energy, and planning to use effectively. The skills in this chapter, on the other hand, are always available and don't have to take more than a few minutes, if that's all the time you have. This means that you can more easily incorporate them in your daily life. Finally, not only will these skills help you manage anxiety, but some of them will also improve your overall health and make you feel better physically. Our physical and mental health are intimately connected. So, improving one will impact the other, and vice versa. Let's get started!

Slow Breathing

When it comes to basic anxiety-management skills, it doesn't get much more basic than breathing, so let's start there. It may be difficult to believe, but how you breathe can have a profound impact on your anxiety and your overall health. There is a lot of research indicating that the simple act of breathing properly (and by *properly*, we mean slow, deep breathing) can reduce anxiety, decrease arousal, and lower your heart rate. Basically, breathing properly can help with relaxation.

So, how do you breathe properly—with slow, deep breaths? Well, one way to begin practicing this skill is simply to slow down your breathing. Deep breathing involves both slowing down your breathing and breathing in a particular way, from your belly, or diaphragm. However, for many people, it can be easiest to start with just focusing on slowing down your breath. The slower you breathe, the more likely it is that your breathing will automatically become deeper. So, slowing your breathing is a great place to start. Now, when it comes to slowing your breathing, you want to focus your attention on your exhalation, or out-breath, in particular. Don't worry about the length or timing of your inhalation, or in-breath. Just focus on extending your out-breath. Let's have you practice this skill right now. You can practice it anywhere and anytime. Find a comfortable position and get started.

Exercise 3.1. Slowing Your Breathing by Extending Your Out-Breath

1. Breathe naturally for a few moments, without trying to change your breath in any way.

2. Count how long it takes you to breathe out each time.

3. Now, focus your attention on gradually lengthening your out-breath.

4. With each breath, focus on extending the out-breath one additional second. For example, if your out-breath was about two seconds to begin with, focus on slowing down your out-breath to three seconds, and then four seconds, and then five seconds, and so on.

5. Keep practicing this exercise and extending the length of your out-breath by one to two seconds with each breath until you have slowed down your breathing to about six to eight breaths per minute.

6. Practice this breathing exercise anytime you notice that you feel anxious or are breathing rapidly.

The great thing about this skill is that it's always available. There is never a time when your breath isn't with you, and the simplicity of this skill makes it the perfect first line of defense when you notice anxiety. So, the next time you're anxious, practice this skill and see how it works.

Deep Breathing

As we mentioned earlier, slowing your breathing isn't the only way to use your breathing to combat anxiety. In fact, one of the most tried-and-true skills for managing anxiety is something called *diaphragmatic breathing*. The diaphragm is the big muscle below your stomach, so diaphragmatic breathing basically just refers to breathing deeply from your belly, rather than your chest. As simple as it sounds, breathing from your diaphragm instead of your chest can have a major impact on your anxiety, as well as your overall arousal.

In fact, breathing from your diaphragm is the natural way to breathe. Everyone starts out breathing this way. Have you ever watched an infant sleep? If so, you may have noticed how deeply infants breathe. Each time they breathe in, their belly expands. As they grow older, however, many people "forget" how to breathe. Rather than breathing deeply from the belly, they start to breathe by expanding their chests and lifting their shoulders. The problem is that breathing this way doesn't give your lungs as much room to expand, resulting in short and shallow breaths. And taking shallow breaths can actually increase your anxiety and arousal— exactly the sensations we are trying to reduce! By breathing with your belly, you give your lungs more room to expand naturally. This slows and deepens your breathing, which naturally brings down arousal and anxiety levels.

So, how do you know if you are using your diaphragm to breathe? Well, one of the simplest strategies for figuring this out is to notice the parts of your body that move as you breathe, paying particular attention to the parts of your body that move in and out or up and down with each breath. If you're breathing properly, your belly should push out when you breathe in and go back in when you breathe out. If your belly expands and contracts as you breathe, you are using your diaphragm to breathe. If, on the other hand, your shoulders move up and down as you breathe, but your belly is still, you're probably breathing from your chest.

Now, as powerful a skill as diaphragmatic breathing can be, it can be challenging to change the way you breathe. Breathing is one of the most automatic things people do, so most of us don't really pay attention to how we breathe. With some practice, however, you can learn how to breathe in a way that reduces your anxiety and puts you one step closer to recovering from PTSD. Remember: breathing from your belly is the natural way of breathing. All you're trying to do is reestablish this natural habit. Use the exercise below (taken from one of our earlier books; Gratz and Chapman 2009) to begin practicing this skill.

When you first practice this exercise, try to do it at a time when you already feel relaxed. It's easier to learn the basic techniques of deep breathing when you're not stressed out.

Exercise 3.2. Practicing Deep Breathing

1. Find a comfortable and quiet place to practice your breathing. Sit up in a chair so that your back is straight and supported.

2. Close your eyes.

3. Put the palm of one of your hands on your stomach and the palm of your other hand on your chest, across your breastbone.

4. Breathe in and out as you normally do. Which hand moves the most when you breathe? The one on your belly or the one on your chest? If the hand on your chest moves and the one on your belly doesn't, this means that you're not breathing with your diaphragm.

5. Now, when you breathe in and out, deliberately push out your belly when you breathe in and let your belly fall when you breathe out. It may feel slightly unnatural at first. This is normal, and this feeling will go away quickly with practice.

6. Continue to breathe in and out. Try to lengthen your breaths. Slowly count to five as you breathe in, and again when you breathe out. Also, try to breathe in through your nose and exhale through your mouth. This may help you take deeper breaths.

7. Practice this breathing exercise a couple of times a day. The more you practice, the more it will become a habit.

Progressive Muscle Relaxation

Another simple skill for managing anxiety is called *progressive muscle relaxation*, or PMR. This is a skill taught in many cognitive-behavioral treatments for anxiety and trauma-related disorders, including PTSD. The basic idea behind this skill is to relax all of the muscle groups in your body. As we discussed in chapter 1, many of the symptoms that go along with PTSD involve tension and arousal. People with PTSD often describe feeling tense, constricted, on edge, and just generally stressed out, and their bodies reflect these feelings. The good news is that because muscle tension is one of the more common side effects of anxiety, relaxing your muscles can help reduce anxiety and can actually help you feel more relaxed in general.

The interesting thing about this skill is that it actually involves tensing your muscles first, before you relax them. There are two reasons for this. First, it can be difficult to just relax your muscles on command. Also, people often don't realize just how tense their muscles are. It can be easy to overlook muscle tension, especially if it has become commonplace for you. If you have a lot of tension in your muscles for an extended period of time, you can become used to those feelings and lose sight of what it's like to not be tense. Therefore, this skill is designed to help you become more aware of muscle tension so that you can then reduce those sensations.

What this skill boils down to is systematically tensing and then relaxing your muscles. It can be helpful to think of your muscles as a pendulum. You can experience greater relaxation and release in your muscles if you tense them first and then relax them. In addition, by tensing your muscles before you relax them, you can become more aware of the difference between these sensations and what it feels like to be tense. Follow the steps below (taken from one of our earlier books; Gratz and Chapman 2009) to begin to practice PMR.

Exercise 3.3. Simple Steps for Practicing Progressive Muscle Relaxation

1. Find a quiet place where you won't be disturbed, and get into a comfortable position. You can do this lying down, sitting up, or even standing up, but you might find that it works best if you're lying down.

2. Next, find a place on your body to start the exercise. Many people find it helpful to start with the top of their head or the tips of their toes.

3. Next, bring your full attention to that part of your body. Let's say that you've started with your forearms. Imagine that your whole head is being drawn down to your forearms. Then, form your hands into fists, squeeze to about 75 to 80 percent of your maximum strength, and hold them tense for about five to ten seconds.

4. Then, let them go and relax your muscles. Notice the difference between how they felt when they were tense and how they feel now. Just notice any sensations of relaxation or warmth, or anything else you might experience.

5. Repeat that process again, first tensing the muscles in your forearms, holding that tension for five to ten seconds, and then relaxing those muscles.

6. Then, move to another area of your body. For instance, you might try your lower legs. Focus your attention on your calf muscles and really try to clench them. Hold this for five to ten

seconds again, and then let it go, relaxing your calves. Repeat this process again to really relax those muscles.

7. Continue going through different muscle groups in your body, doing exactly the same thing. Each time, just tense your muscles about 75 percent to 80 percent for about five to ten seconds, and then relax them, focusing on the difference you feel.

Do PMR for anywhere from five to twenty-five minutes, depending on how much time you have. Doing it for even five minutes can make a difference. So, try it out and see how much better you feel.

One particularly useful thing about this skill is that you can personalize it to make it work best for you. Although exercise 3.3 walked you through how to use this skill to help reduce muscle tension throughout your body, anxiety affects everyone differently. The areas of your body where you carry your anxiety (or the particular muscles that tense the most when you're anxious) may be different from those of other people. Therefore, one way to get the most from this skill is to figure out the areas of your body where you experience the most tension when you're anxious. Do you feel tension in your neck or shoulders? Or in your lower or upper back? What about in your head? See if you can notice the areas of your body that are most tense when you're anxious, and if you do, practice this skill specifically on those areas. This will help you focus the skill exactly where you need it the most.

Mindfulness

Another basic skill for managing anxiety is to practice observing the bodily sensations, thoughts, and urges that go along with anxiety in a nonjudgmental and nonreactive way; in other words, observing your anxiety mindfully. One reason anxiety can be so disruptive is that it tends to capture our attention in a way that makes it difficult to take a step back from our experience.

Consider what happens when you feel intense anxiety. Do you find it easy to focus your attention on other things, or do you find your attention pulled to the physical sensations you're experiencing or the worries going through your mind? For many people, feelings of anxiety (and the thoughts and physical sensations that accompany these feelings) become the sole focus of attention, which can lead to even more anxiety. Getting caught up in anxiety can create a vicious cycle of ever-increasing anxiety or panic, particularly when those feelings are judged as dangerous or threatening. This process is common among people with PTSD. It is no surprise that people with PTSD experience a high level of worry (Tull et al. 2011) and are at greater risk for experiencing panic attacks (Falsetti and Resnick 1997).

Mindfulness can help you combat this vicious cycle by allowing you to notice your anxiety without getting caught up in the experience or reacting to it. Rather than getting swept up in your anxiety or anxiety-related thoughts, this skill will help you take one step back from your experience so that you can simply observe your anxiety, without getting stuck in it. The goal isn't to avoid your anxiety or get rid of it; in fact, mindfulness will actually help you become more aware of your emotions. Instead, the goal of this skill is just to notice all of the different parts of your anxiety, without trying to push them away or cling to them.

To practice this skill, simply pay attention to the bodily sensations, thoughts, and action urges that go along with anxiety, watching each of these experiences arise and pass from one moment to the next. You may want to start by bringing your attention to how the anxiety feels in your body and the different sensations you're experiencing. Then, bring your attention to the thoughts that are present and any urges you're experiencing to act in a particular way. If you find yourself getting caught up in your thoughts or your desires to act in a certain way, gently turn your attention back to how the emotion feels in your body.

The exercise below provides some simple step-by-step instructions for beginning to pay attention to your anxiety without judgment, evaluation, or attachment. The next time you feel anxious, try it out and see how it works.

Exercise 3.4. Mindfully Observing Your Anxiety

1. To begin, find a comfortable and quiet place where you can sit or lie down.

2. Close your eyes.

3. Focus your attention on your breathing. Notice what it feels like to breathe in and breathe out. Notice what parts of your body move as you breathe in and out.

4. Next, bring your attention to your body and notice where in your body you feel the anxiety. Scan your body from head to toe, paying attention to the sensations in each part of your body as you go. Spend about ten seconds on each area of your body, just stepping back in your mind, paying attention, and noticing your sensations.

5. Once you have finished scanning your body, bring your attention to the parts of your body where you feel your anxiety. Zero in on the sensations of anxiety. Watch them rise and fall as you would watch a wave in the ocean cresting and then crashing onto the shore.

6. If you notice that you are labeling or judging those senstions, notice that evaluation or thought, and then bring your attention back to simply noticing the sensations as just sensations.

7. Next, bring your attention to any thoughts that are present, focusing on just noticing these thoughts as thoughts, without attaching to them. If you find that you start getting caught up in your thoughts or start judging yourself for having these thoughts, just notice that experience and bring your attention back to simply noticing the thoughts that are present.

8. Now see if you can bring your attention to any action urges you are experiencing, noticing urges to act in any way. Focus on just noticing these urges as they rise and fall, bringing attention to the ways they change or stay the same.

9. Keep focusing on the different components of your anxiety without escaping or avoiding them. Focus on just noticing your experiences, without trying to push them away or change them in any way. Do this for ten to fifteen minutes, or until the emotion subsides.

Another way to begin practicing this skill is to think about a recent time when you felt anxiety. Not only will this give you a chance to practice this skill at any time (even if you aren't currently feeling anxious), it will allow you to choose an experience of anxiety that wasn't too intense. Although mindfulness can be helpful at any time, many people find it easier to begin practicing this skill when anxiety isn't too intense. It's a lot like learning to ride a bike. You wouldn't start off by practicing on rough terrain or a steep hill. Instead, you'd learn to ride on a smooth, flat surface, away from traffic. Skills for managing anxiety and other PTSD symptoms work the same way—we recommend beginning to practice these skills when symptoms are less intense. This will give you the chance to learn the basics of these skills before applying them to more challenging situations.

Exercise

Another simple yet powerful strategy for managing anxiety is exercise. More and more research is showing that exercise is a great way to reduce anxiety and its effects on the body (Asmundson et al. 2013; Powers, Asmundson, and Smits 2015). In fact, there's even some evidence that exercise can reduce the symptoms of PTSD in particular (Fetzner and Asmundson 2015; Manger and Motta 2005). Not only does regular exercise make your body stronger and increase the physical resources available to you, but it can also help alleviate tension and anxiety in the moment. In addition, regular exercise can lead to improvements in sleep, mood, and confidence (Asmundson et al. 2013)—all of which are important for people with PTSD.

Exercise can also be thought of as a form of exposure to the bodily sensations that go along with anxiety, such as increased heart rate, shortness of breath, or muscle tension. As we mentioned in chapter 1, exposure is one of the best treatments for PTSD, and exposure to these types of bodily sensations has been found to be helpful for people with PTSD (Wald and Taylor 2007). PTSD can make people more sensitive to and afraid of these types of sensations. Although these sensations are harmless in and of themselves, they can be interpreted as a sign of a nearby threat or impending panic attack. As a result, some people with PTSD grow to fear these sensations and what they could mean. This fear can then lead to efforts to avoid these sensations or prevent them from occurring, such as by avoiding physical activity or misusing prescription drugs. Exercise, on the other hand, can counteract this avoidance and teach you that these sensations are not dangerous. Exposing yourself to these feared sensations through exercise can increase your comfort level with these sensations and make you less likely to try to avoid them.

The good news is that getting regular exercise doesn't necessarily mean working out at the gym several times a week. Going to the gym is one way to get exercise, but there are many other ways to get exercise that don't require a gym. The anxiety-reducing benefits of exercise can be achieved by doing any sort of moderate physical activity for thirty minutes a day for five days a week. And this doesn't have to mean running or using exercise equipment. It could mean walking, gardening, vacuuming, walking up the stairs at your residence or place of work, or anything else that gets your heart rate up. The only thing that matters is that you do something moderately active for at least thirty minutes.

So, focus on getting activity anywhere you can. If you have to go to the store, park as far away as possible so you can get in a bit of a walk. If you work in a multiple-story building or have appointments in buildings like that, take the stairs rather than the elevator. If you need to clean your house, focus on making the cleaning as physical as possible, moving the vacuum vigorously and really throwing yourself into scrubbing the floors or polishing the furniture. The goal is simply to get your heart rate up and your body moving for thirty minutes. How you go about this is completely up to you.

Now, this probably isn't the first time you've heard that exercise is good for you. Even though it's now common knowledge that exercise is important, many people struggle to incorporate exercise into their daily routine. There are all kinds of things that can get in the way and make it difficult to follow through with even the best of intentions. The good news is that there are some simple strategies you can use to increase commitment to an exercise plan and make it more likely that you'll stick with it.

1. Schedule your exercise time in advance, and stick with the time you chose. Thinking that you'll just squeeze in exercise when you have time makes it less likely you'll follow through with it. The idea behind committing to an exercise plan is to make it a priority—something you actually schedule into your daily routine. If you wait until you have the time, you probably won't find it. Scheduling a time guarantees that the time will be available.

2. Be creative in your exercise plan. The more flexible and creative you are about how to get exercise, the more options you'll have for incorporating exercise into your daily routine. If the only place you exercise is the gym, you may find it difficult to exercise on days when you get home from work late. If running is your only form of exercise, stormy weather or extremes in temperature could get in the way. The more options you have for exercise, the more likely it is that one of these will work on any given day. An added benefit of having a number of options for exercise is that you're less likely to get bored.

3. Focus your attention on the benefits of exercise and why you committed to an exercise plan to begin with. It's easier to not follow through with something if we forget why it's important and what it will do for us. And if you're struggling with PTSD, anything you can do to reduce anxiety is going to have a huge impact on your life. So, focus on all of the benefits of exercise and how you'll feel as you start to manage your anxiety. Write out these benefits and carry this list with you to give you motivation to exercise even when you're busy or feeling tired. It can also help to track how you feel before and after you exercise, to help you connect with the benefits of exercise for your mood and anxiety.

Use exercise 3.5 to track your anxiety levels before and after you exercise. This will help you connect with the benefits of exercise, as well as the forms of exercise that are most beneficial for you.

To use this worksheet, first fill in the day, starting time, and specific exercise you plan to do. Next, rate the intensity of your anxiety on a scale from 0 (no anxiety at all) to 100 (the most intense anxiety ever) and put your rating in the column labeled "Anxiety Before." Once you have finished exercising, enter the ending time and then immediately rate your anxiety again on a scale from 0 to 100 in the "Anxiety After" column. This will help you figure out the impact of different forms of exercise on your anxiety.

At the bottom of the exercise is a section where you can write any comments you have about your experiences. Use this section to take notes on the exercises that seem to work the best for you and any ideas you have about what you might do the next time you want to reduce your anxiety through exercise.

Exercise 3.5. Tracking the Benefits of Exercise

Day	Start Time	End Time	Exercise	Anxiety Before (0–100)	Anxiety After (0–100)

Comments

Moving Forward

This chapter focused on basic skills for managing anxiety, including slow and deep breathing, PMR, mindfulness, and exercise. These are some of the foundational skills for managing anxiety. They also have the benefit of being available to you at all times—no planning or special equipment needed!

Now that you've learned these skills, it's time to try them out and see how they work. The more you practice these skills, the easier they will become, and the more natural they will feel. And if you incorporate these skills into your daily life, you may even start to notice that you feel less anxious overall.

CHAPTER 4

Managing Intrusive and Other Negative Thoughts

Unpleasant thoughts are a central feature of PTSD and can take a number of different forms. One of the most common is intrusive memories about a traumatic event. Not only are these memories unpleasant in and of themselves, but they are also often easily triggered and can occur unexpectedly. In some cases, these memories can be so strong that it may even feel as if the traumatic event were happening again. As a result of these experiences, many people with PTSD begin to fear their own thoughts and go to great lengths to try to avoid activities, situations, people, places, or things that bring up these memories. In addition to these intrusive thoughts about the traumatic event itself, many people with PTSD develop negative beliefs about themselves, other people, and the world. These beliefs tend to be extreme and black-or-white, such as *I will never be safe again* or *It was all my fault*. They also commonly center on themes involving a lack of safety, helplessness, hopelessness, and self-blame. These types of beliefs can bring up feelings of fear, anxiety, anger, sadness, guilt, and shame. They may also increase your desire to avoid certain places, situations, or people, which can then make these beliefs (and other PTSD symptoms) stronger.

Because intrusive memories and negative beliefs can be so painful and difficult to manage, it's common for people to try to cope with these thoughts by simply pushing them away or avoiding them (Purdon 1999). Although this may work initially to some extent, it can cause more problems for you in the long run. First, it can take a lot of effort to try to push away unpleasant thoughts, especially if they are triggered a lot. This can take your attention away from other important parts of your life. It may also leave you with less energy to deal with other symptoms of PTSD or life in general. Second, pushing away your thoughts can lead to something called the *rebound effect*. Even though you may be successful in pushing away thoughts for a short period of time, these thoughts will eventually come back and may be even stronger when they do

(Shipherd and Beck 2005). It is kind of like trying to keep a beach ball under water. It is difficult to do, and when the ball slides out of your grip, it often pops up to the surface with a lot of force.

Given how painful and disruptive these negative thoughts can be, it's important to learn a number of different strategies for responding to them effectively. The good news is that most treatments that are helpful for PTSD include skills for managing distressing or intrusive thoughts. In this chapter, we cover several skills from dialectical behavior therapy, acceptance and commitment therapy, and cognitive processing therapy that may help you better cope with intrusive thoughts and negative beliefs, as well as reduce their power over you, your emotions, and your behaviors.

Being Mindful of Thoughts

Mindfulness can be a particularly helpful way of dealing with negative thoughts and beliefs. Because intrusive memories can occur unexpectedly and be so upsetting, they can quickly grab your attention and pull you into the past. When this happens, you may be flooded with terror and find it difficult to take a step back from those thoughts. PTSD can also lead to negative thoughts or judgments about yourself. You may blame yourself for the traumatic event or judge yourself as weak because you haven't been able to recover from what happened. Thoughts like this can then lead to shame, guilt, sadness, and anger, which can make your judgments of yourself feel true. In the end, however, no matter how real or true they feel, these are just thoughts and just a symptom of your PTSD. Just as mindfulness can be a helpful strategy for managing anxiety symptoms of PTSD, it can also be useful for managing the intrusive thoughts and negative beliefs that go along with PTSD. To review, mindfulness skills involve focusing on the present moment, controlling your attention, and observing and describing your experience in a nonjudgmental and nonreactive manner. There are several mindfulness skills that can be helpful for managing these thoughts.

Mindfully Observing Thoughts

One of the best strategies for managing negative thoughts is to simply notice your thoughts without attaching to, reacting to, or acting on these thoughts (Linehan 1993a, 2015). In dialectical behavior therapy (Linehan 1993b, 2015), this specific skill is called "Teflon mind." Basically, the idea is to allow thoughts to slide out of your mind in the same way that the nonstick Teflon coating on pans allows food to slide out of the pan when you are done cooking. Have you ever tried making an omelet or cooking a piece of fish in a pan that did not have a Teflon coating? The food tends to stick to the bottom of the pan. The same rules apply to our minds. If we don't practice having a Teflon mind, troublesome thoughts, whether they are memories of a traumatic event or judgments about ourselves, tend to stick to our minds rather than sliding out, as thoughts that are not distressing tend to do. So, the goal of this mindfulness skill is to allow your PTSD-related thoughts to pass in and out of your mind without getting stuck to them.

One way to do this is to picture placing each of the thoughts going through your mind on a conveyor belt (adapted from the *Skills Training Manual for Treating Borderline Personality Disorder;* Linehan 1993b). Conveyor belts tend to operate at a steady speed, moving objects slowly across a room. In the same way, you can picture all of your thoughts moving slowly and steadily across your mind. Don't try to change the speed of the conveyor belt or take thoughts off the conveyor belt. Just notice each thought passing through your mind, one after another. If you notice that the conveyor belt stalls or that the thoughts start piling up on one another on the belt or the thoughts start falling off the belt, just notice that experience and gently turn your attention back to the conveyor belt, placing each thought on the belt and noticing as it moves through your mind. Practice this exercise for at least five minutes once a day.

There are all kinds of ways to practice this skill, and all kinds of imagery you can use. Rather than placing your thoughts on a conveyor belt, you can place them on leaves floating down a stream, clouds floating across a sky, or balloons being released into the air. Use whatever imagery works best for you. It doesn't matter what imagery you use as long as you practice placing your thoughts on an object and noticing them pass.

Labeling Thoughts as Thoughts

Another mindfulness skill that can be helpful in dealing with distressing memories or negative beliefs is the dialectical behavior therapy mindfulness skill of labeling your experience (Linehan 1993b). One of the reasons human beings tend to get so attached to and caught up in our thoughts is that we buy into these thoughts as literally true. Rather than recognizing that our thoughts are simply thoughts generated by our minds that may or may not be accurate, we believe them and take them to be the truth. Therefore, labeling a thought as just a thought is one way to keep yourself from getting caught up in your thoughts. This skill will help you recognize that no matter how intense or real your thoughts may seem, they are not a premonition of things to come or an accurate indication of how things are. So the next time you have a distressing thought, make sure to label it as just a thought that your mind has generated. For example, if you notice yourself thinking *I am weak* or *The world is full of danger,* say to yourself something like *I am having the thought that I am weak* or *I am having the thought that the world is full of danger.* Approaching your negative thoughts in this way and clearly labeling them as thoughts will help you take a step back from them and not buy into them as if they were literally true.

Exercise 4.1 is designed to help you with this. In the space provided, write down all of the negative thoughts that you struggle with the most. Try to focus on any negative beliefs about yourself, others, or the world that developed after you experienced your traumatic event. Acknowledging these thoughts as just thoughts will take away some of their power and help you connect with the fact that they are just thoughts generated by your mind. After you have written down your most troublesome thoughts on the worksheet below, reflect on how prefacing them with the statement "I am having the thought that…" changes your experience of these thoughts.

Exercise 4.1. Labeling Your Negative Thoughts as Just Thoughts

I am having the thought that _____

_____.

I am having the thought that _____

_____.

I am having the thought that _____

_____.

I am having the thought that _____

_____.

I am having the thought that _____

_____.

I am having the thought that _____

_____.

I am having the thought that _____

_____.

Connecting with the Present Moment

Another way that mindfulness can be helpful in managing intrusive thoughts and memories in PTSD is by helping you refocus your attention on the present moment. Intrusive thoughts in PTSD distract you from the present moment by pulling you into the past or the future. They can be so vivid that you may feel as if the traumatic event is happening again (that is, you may experience a flashback). Alternatively, intrusive thoughts may make you feel like you aren't safe, leading you to worry about the future. Rather than getting caught up in these thoughts, the goal of this skill is to focus your attention on observing and describing whatever you are doing at that moment. This will keep you connected to the present moment, rather than getting caught up in memories of the past or worries about the future. This skill is similar to the grounding skills you practiced to cope with triggers in exercise 2.6 and 2.7 of chapter 2. Exercise 4.2 has a list of questions to help you fully connect with the present moment. Ask yourself these questions the next time you notice yourself getting caught up in intrusive thoughts about the past or future, or just feeling a bit distracted. It can be helpful to get into the habit of practicing this skill and connecting to the present moment before intrusive thoughts arise.

Exercise 4.2. Questions to Help You Connect with the Present Moment

What do I see around me right now?_____

_____

What objects, people, or situations do I observe?_____

_____

What am I hearing right now? Are the sounds loud or soft? Nearby or far away?_____

_____

What do I feel against my skin? What temperatures and textures do I notice?_____

_____

How does my body feel? Are my muscles relaxed or tense?_____

_____

What scents do I smell currently? Are they subtle or more obvious? Pleasant or unpleasant? Where are they coming from? _____

_____

_____

Once you've refocused your attention on your experiences in the present moment, concentrate on throwing yourself completely into whatever you are doing. The more that you can focus all of your attention on what you are doing in the moment, the less likely you are to get caught up in negative thoughts. Remember: mindfulness is about connecting with the present moment and bringing all of your attention to whatever you are doing. So use this skill to get out of your head and immerse yourself in your experiences, connecting with them completely. This can help pull you out of the past or the future. It can also help you connect with the moment as it is, as opposed to how your mind interprets it. By keeping you grounded in the present moment, this skill will also help you get the most out of what you are doing and fully connect with your life. So the next time you notice that you are getting caught up in intrusive thoughts about the past or future, practice bringing your full attention and awareness back to whatever you are doing at the time.

Defusing from Thoughts

Have you ever noticed that when negative beliefs or memories of your traumatic event come up, they quickly lead to other thoughts and emotions? Think of your mind as a spiderweb. Every thought that comes up is connected to many other thoughts or images, and all of those are connected to others (and sometimes to each other). For example, when you hear the word *chocolate*, what immediately comes to mind? You may think of chocolate ice cream, the color brown, chocolate cake, hot chocolate, or times when chocolate would be served, such as Valentine's Day. You may even notice your mouth watering a little. Due to the experiences you have had in your life, a number of different thoughts, feelings, and experiences have become connected to or associated with the word *chocolate* in your mind.

The same rules apply when you think of a traumatic event or have a negative belief enter your mind. It quickly leads to other unpleasant thoughts and feelings that are associated with that event or belief. As this cycle continues, we can get stuck in a cycle of overwhelming negative thoughts and feelings. Fortunately, there are ways of breaking the bonds that connect these experiences. This can be done using a cognitive defusion exercise from acceptance and commitment therapy (Hayes, Strosahl, and Wilson 2011). They use the term *cognitive defusion* because the exercise helps reduce the power of your thoughts by reducing the extent to which you fuse or connect with that thought. This prevents that thought from activating other parts of your mind's spiderweb. The exercise is quite simple but very effective. Let's try it with the chocolate example. Say *chocolate* out loud. Notice all the other thoughts and feelings that come up when you say *chocolate*? Now, as fast as you can, say *chocolate* over and over again. With each utterance of *chocolate*, try to say it faster and faster. Do this for at least thirty seconds.

What did you notice? Did you notice at some point that the word *chocolate* sounded like gibberish? You likely also noticed that as you said the word faster and faster, all of the things that you associate with chocolate began to fall away. The bonds connecting the things you associate with chocolate were broken, because you were taking the meaning away from the word by turning it into a nonsense sound. You can use this same skill with trauma-related thoughts or negative beliefs. Try to reduce the thought or belief into one or two words. Notice all of the other thoughts and feelings that arise, and then say the word over and over again as quickly as you can. You should notice the power of that thought or belief decrease. This can be a helpful strategy when these thoughts and beliefs become sticky—that is, when they grab your attention and refuse to let go.

Managing Negative Beliefs

As we mentioned in chapter 1, as well as earlier in this chapter, the experience of a traumatic event can alter the way in which you view yourself, other people, and the world. We all view the world through filters. How our filter operates is largely influenced by our life experiences, and it helps us understand and organize all of the information that we take in. For example, let's say that you believe that people are inherently good. While walking down the street one day, you see someone you know from work across the way. You wave to him, but he doesn't wave back. How do you make sense of his behavior? If you believe that people are inherently good, you will likely think that he just didn't see you. He would have waved back if he'd seen you. Now, if you believe the opposite—that people are inherently bad—you will be more likely to interpret his behavior as rudeness—clearly he was rejecting you. Your filter about how people generally operate in the world influenced your evaluation of his behavior. And this interpretation is then going to influence the emotions you experience and how you might behave the next time you see him.

Most of us start out with positive or balanced beliefs about ourselves and the world around us. A traumatic event, however, can provide strong evidence against these beliefs. You are then placed in a position where your filters have to be reworked in order to make this new information fit. This can go a few different ways. You might modify your beliefs—*For the most part, people are inherently good* or *People are inherently good but sometimes do bad things*. Your original belief has been changed somewhat to take account of the new information. The original belief is still there, but some additional information is included that recognizes there are exceptions to your original rule. This is called *accommodation*, and in cognitive processing therapy for PTSD, it is what one is striving for after the experience of a traumatic event (Resick, Monson, and Chard 2008).

For many people, however, a traumatic event causes their beliefs to shift toward the other extreme—*All people are inherently bad*. This extreme thought can serve an important function after a traumatic event. It will likely keep you from getting too close to people and make you avoid certain situations, increasing your sense of safety and control. In the long term, however, this belief is going to interfere with the development of meaningful relationships and may increase the extent to which you feel detached or disconnected from others. Finally, instead of developing extreme beliefs after a traumatic event, some people try to make the new information fit their original belief. For example, you may think that, *People are inherently good, so I must have done something terribly wrong*. This approach to making sense of a traumatic event often leads to self-blame, guilt, and shame. It is also possible that a traumatic event may confirm and strengthen previously held negative beliefs.

These negative beliefs can stall recovery from a traumatic event and PTSD. This is why they are called *stuck points* in cognitive processing therapy (Resick, Monson, and Chard 2008). These beliefs can lead to a wide variety of unpleasant emotions that can interfere with your ability to work through the emotions that stem directly from your traumatic event. Think about it—let's say that you experienced the unexpected and violent death of a loved one. It is going to be difficult to work through the sadness and anger associated with your loss if these emotions are muddied by the guilt you feel due to the belief that you could have done something to prevent your loved one's death. These beliefs can also drive avoidance or other unhealthy behavior. For this reason, a central goal of cognitive processing therapy is identifying these stuck points and problematic patterns of thinking, as well as developing more balanced and flexible beliefs (that is, accommodation) (Resick, Monson, and Chard 2008).

Identifying Stuck Points

To begin to identify negative beliefs that developed after your traumatic event, it can be helpful to write an *impact statement* (Resick, Monson, and Chard 2008) This is basically a description of how your traumatic event changed the way you view yourself, other people, and the world (Resick, Monson, and Chard 2008).

Exercise 4.3 will help you write your impact statement. On a sheet of paper, write your answers to the questions in the exercise below. Try to write at least one page. You *do not* need to write about what happened during your traumatic event. Those details are not required. Also, make sure you do this exercise at a time when you have some privacy and the ability to sit with and express any emotions that may come up while you are writing. Finally, it is best for this exercise to be handwritten—with pen and paper. Writing with pen and paper helps you more fully engage with the exercise. Don't worry about grammar, spelling, or neatness. The most important thing is that you connect with and write about your thoughts and feelings associated with your traumatic event.

Exercise 4.3. Writing an Impact Statement

1. Why do you think your traumatic event happened to you?

   _____

   _____

   _____

2. In general, how do you think your traumatic event changed the way you think about or see yourself, other people, and the world?

   _____

   _____

   _____

If you are having a hard time identifying ways in which your traumatic event changed your beliefs about yourself, others, and the world, it may be helpful to think about the ways in which your traumatic event affected your views on specific aspects of your life:

• safety

• trust

- control

- self-esteem

- intimacy

Once you have written your impact statement, read over it and try to identify your negative beliefs that developed or were strengthened after experiencing your traumatic event. Write them down in exercise 4.4 below. It's fine if you are able to identify only one negative belief. There is no need to fill out all lines in the exercise. If you are finding it difficult to identify your negative beliefs, consider the following common negative beliefs that can develop after a traumatic event:

- No one can be trusted.

- I will never be truly safe.

- The world is a dangerous place.

- I am unlovable.

- I am permanently damaged.

- I am a bad person.

- People are only out for themselves.

- Life is unfair.

- I will never recover.

- There is nothing I can do to change my situation.

Exercise 4.4. List Your Negative Beliefs or Stuck Points

Stuck Point 1: _____

Stuck Point 2: _____

Stuck Point 3: _____

Stuck Point 4: _____

Stuck Point 5: _____

Stuck Point 6: _____

Stuck Point 7: _____

Stuck Point 8: _____

Stuck Point 9: _____

Stuck Point 10: _____

After identifying your stuck points, it can be helpful to think about what kind of situations tend to bring up these beliefs, what emotions stem from these beliefs, and how they influence your behavior. Try to remember a recent time when each of the negative beliefs in exercise 4.4 came up for you. Write down that belief in the second column of exercise 4.5 below. Then, write down the situation that brought up that negative belief. How did you feel after having that thought? Finally, write down how you responded to that situation.

For example, in the first column, you might write, "My partner was late for our dinner date." This event may have brought up the belief that you are not important or that no one cares about you. These beliefs perhaps resulted in emotions of anger and sadness, which then led to your lashing out at your partner.

Exercise 4.5. Connecting Situations, Thoughts, Feelings, and Behavior

Situation	Negative Belief or Stuck Point	Emotion	How Did You Respond?

Identifying your negative beliefs and when they tend to come up is the first step in addressing them. This helps you to be on the lookout for them, so you can begin to modify how you approach and buy into them, using some of the skills discussed throughout this chapter. In addition, this exercise can help you better recognize the connection between situations, thoughts, emotions, and behavior. Doing so can reduce the extent to which your thoughts and emotions feel as though they come out of the blue, bringing about a greater sense of predictability and understanding when it comes to your internal experience.

Generating Alternatives

Once you feel that you have a good idea of your negative beliefs, it is time to change the way you relate to those thoughts. Basically, you want to take steps to decrease the believability of those thoughts. There are a number of different skills that you can use to do this. Mindfully observing thoughts, labeling thoughts as thoughts, and the cognitive defusion exercise from acceptance and commitment therapy may all be useful in helping you take a step back from your negative beliefs and reducing the extent to which you buy into them. It can also be helpful to challenge these beliefs. That is, you can play the role of a detective or lawyer and gather evidence to show that these thoughts are not providing you with an accurate or complete picture of how things really are.

Questioning Your Negative Beliefs

The human mind likes order and consistency. Therefore, when you have a negative belief, you will be more likely to notice or evaluate things in such a way that they confirm that belief. In addition, negative beliefs can lead to emotions and behaviors that may also confirm them. Take the example of the partner who was late for the dinner date. If your beliefs led you to lash out at your partner for being late, it is possible that your partner would respond with anger as well. This may then further strengthen the thought *No one cares about me*. However, just because a thought *feels* true, it does not mean that it is true. If you gather enough information, you typically can find evidence that disconfirms your negative belief or at least helps you come up with a more balanced and realistic evaluation of it.

Another skill from cognitive processing therapy (Resick, Monson, and Chard 2008) that can be helpful in reducing the power of your negative beliefs is questioning those beliefs. Exercise 4.6 takes you through some questions that will help you gather evidence for and against your beliefs. In doing so, you can reduce the extent to which you buy into your negative beliefs as complete and total truth. As you go through this exercise and find evidence counter to your beliefs, make sure you come up with evidence that you think other people would agree with. Basically, imagine that you are in a courtroom and that your negative belief is on the stand. You want evidence that is reasonable and would hold up in court.

In the exercise, write down the negative belief you would like to work on. Then try to answer the questions that follow. Some questions may not be relevant to your negative belief, so focus on the ones that you think apply. Try to provide as much information as you can to answer each question.

Exercise 4.6. Questioning Your Negative Beliefs

Negative Belief/Stuck Point: _____

1. What evidence do you have that supports this thought? What about evidence that goes against this thought? Try to come up with as much evidence against this thought as you can.

    _____

    _____

2. What evidence do you have that this thought is only occurring out of habit?

    _____

    _____

3. Is this a black-or-white thought? That is, is it focused on one extreme (look for words like *never*, *always*, and *must*)? Is there any gray area?

    _____

    _____

4. In evaluating the situation, are you considering all possibilities or explanations for what occurred? What are some other alternative explanations?

    _____

    _____

5. Are you taking into account everything that happened in the situation, or are you focusing on only one small part?

_____

_____

6. Do you think your feelings about what happened are influencing your thoughts about the situation and what it means? If so, what facts do you have about the situation and how do these fit with or go against your beliefs?

_____

_____

7. Are you evaluating the situation based on what you know now instead of what you knew at the time (this is called *hindsight bias*)?

_____

_____

8. What would you tell a friend if this situation had happened to him or her?

_____

_____

Repeat this exercise for each negative belief that you have. There are definitely other questions you could ask, so feel free to come up with other questions that you think could be helpful in questioning your negative beliefs. In this exercise, you are looking at your thoughts from a number of different perspectives. By seeing that you can view a situation or experience from all angles, you can reduce the believability of your negative beliefs. It can also increase your flexibility in dealing with a situation. With each new perspective, there are more ways of responding to a situation in a healthy and effective way. Finally, this exercise can show that you don't have to take your beliefs at face value. Just because they may feel true doesn't necessarily mean that they are true.

Checking the Facts

Another skill that may be useful for managing negative beliefs is the dialectical behavior therapy skill of checking the facts (Linehan 2015). This skill is particularly useful when you find yourself buying into extreme or catastrophic interpretations about the world or other people, and just can't take a step back from these thoughts. The goal of this skill is to separate the facts of the situation—what you can actually observe—from your interpretations of those facts by identifying and labeling your interpretations as just that. Noticing the interpretations that are present and identifying them as such is one of the best strategies for taking a step back from these thoughts. Once you've connected with the fact that an interpretation is just an interpretation, it's far easier to detach from that thought and use some of the exercises described at the beginning of this chapter. Similar to the previous exercise on questioning your beliefs, checking the facts can also assist you in coming up with more accurate interpretations of your situation. So the next time you find yourself getting caught up in extreme or catastrophic interpretations, bring your attention back to just the facts of the situation and see if you can separate those facts from your interpretations and opinions. Use exercise 4.7 to practice this skill.

Exercise 4.7. Steps for Checking the Facts and Identifying Interpretations

1. Write a description of the situation that is prompting your negative thoughts. Describe it as you would to a friend or loved one.

_____

_____

_____

_____

_____

2. Go through this description and see if you can identify any interpretations that are present. Focus on identifying anything in your description that moves beyond what you can actually see and hear. If you didn't actually observe it, it is probably an interpretation. Circle any that you find.

3. Now that you've identified the interpretations in your initial written description, label those as interpretations in the lines below.

    I am having the interpretation that _____

    _____.

    I am having the interpretation that _____

    _____.

    I am having the interpretation that _____

    _____.

    I am having the interpretation that _____

    _____.

    I am having the interpretation that _____

    _____.

4. Finally, rewrite your description by focusing on just the facts of the situation and what you can actually observe.

    _____

    _____

    _____

    _____

    _____

    _____

Identifying Unhelpful Thinking Habits

When you were doing exercise 4.5, you may have noticed that you tend to evaluate situations in certain ways. For example, you may have noticed that whenever you feel anxious, you assume it is because you have done something wrong. Or you may have noticed that whenever you see someone who reminds you of your perpetrator, you assume that person is dangerous. The way we respond to situations can largely occur out of habit. Our response isn't based on the information we have about the new situation we are facing, but instead, it is based on our experiences from the past. Cognitive processing therapy recognizes that this can lead to the frequent occurrence of unpleasant emotions and maladaptive, unhealthy, or self-defeating behavior (such as not leaving the house due to the idea that you can never be safe) (Resick, Monson, and Chard 2008). Therefore, it can be helpful to bring awareness to these negative thought patterns. Just as it is important to bring awareness to single negative beliefs, knowing your negative thinking patterns can make it easier to step back from your experience and to use the other strategies we discussed in this chapter.

There are a number of types of unhelpful thinking patterns th at people can experience. Exercise 4.8 describes several of these, along with an example of each. Some of these come from cognitive processing therapy (Resick, Monson, and Chard 2008) and others come from cognitive therapy in general (Beck 1995). Think about the unhelpful patterns of thinking that you tend to fall into and how they affect your emotions and your behavior. For example, if you have a tendency to focus on the worst-case scenario as the likely outcome for any given situation, you may notice that this thought leads you to give up or isolate. If you have a tendency to mind read, this might lead you to lash out at others. Given that these unhelpful thinking patterns often occur outside our awareness, it may be helpful to spend some time thinking back about your week or to take a couple of days monitoring your thoughts and behavior. It may also be useful to think about times when you engaged in a maladaptive or unhealthy behavior and then work backward from that point to see if you can remember any negative thoughts or evaluations that might have driven that behavior.

Exercise 4.8. Identifying Unhelpful Thinking Patterns

1. Jumping to conclusions about what happened.

   How did this affect your behavior? What did you do? _____

   _____

   Example: *That man didn't make eye contact with me. He must be up to no good.*

2. Blowing things out of proportion or minimizing the importance of a situation.

   How did this affect your behavior? What did you do? _____

   _____

   Example: *I was in the hospital for only a day after my accident, whereas others were much more seriously hurt. I shouldn't be feeling the way I am. I need to just suck it up and stop being so weak.*

3. Tunnel vision, or focusing only on negative parts of a situation or event.

   How did this affect your behavior? What did you do? _____

   _____

   Example: *Nothing good or positive has ever happened to me. My life is horrible.*

4. Catastrophizing, or focusing on the worst-case scenario.

   How did this affect your behavior? What did you do? _____

   _____

   Example: *My boss wants to meet with me. I know it is because I messed up; she wants to fire me. I am going to be broke and without a job.*

5. Thinking that something bad that happened to you in the past is evidence that bad things will keep happening to you.

How did this affect your behavior? What did you do? _____

_____

Example: *I was assaulted when I went on a date with a man. I can never go on a date again, as this will happen again. Men can't be trusted.*

6. Mind reading, or assuming you know what people are thinking.

    How did this affect your behavior? What did you do? _____

    _____

    Example: *She couldn't get coffee with me. It must be because she thinks I am annoying. She must not be able to stand being around me.*

7. Basing your evaluation of a situation solely on your emotions.

    How did this affect your behavior? What did you do? _____

    _____

    Example: *I am feeling scared. Something bad is about to happen to me.*

8. Thinking that you are responsible for things that really are out of your control (for example, how others act, think, or feel).

    How did this affect your behavior? What did you do? _____

    _____

    Example: *My husband hit me. I must have done something wrong. It's my fault.*

9. Black-or-white thinking.

    How did this affect your behavior? What did you do? _____

    _____

    Example: *If I don't say or do just the right things on this interview, it is going to be a complete failure.*

After you have identified your unhelpful thinking patterns, try to think about upcoming situations where these patterns may occur. Then plan ahead. Looking back over the skills discussed in this chapter, what skills could you use? For some thoughts, coming up with alternatives or checking the facts might be the best way of addressing the problem. In other situations, being mindful of the present moment may help put you in *beginner's mind*, or connecting with the present moment as it is as opposed to how our mind tells us it is. Simply telling yourself *This is just a thought, and it is occurring only out of habit* may also help reduce the influence of your unhelpful thinking patterns over your behavior.

Moving Forward

Unpleasant thoughts and memories are common and central symptoms of PTSD. These intrusive thoughts can make it feel as though there is no escape from your traumatic event. And the negative beliefs that develop can make you feel as though there is no way to recover. This is why it is incredibly important to learn ways of coping with these experiences and using skills to reduce their power over you. This chapter focused on skills for managing the unpleasant thoughts, memories, and beliefs that commonly go along with PTSD. These skills include mindfully observing your thoughts without attaching to them, focusing your attention on the present moment and throwing yourself into whatever you are doing, and identifying alternative ways of thinking that may be more useful and effective for you.

You may be thinking that there are a lot of skills in this chapter. That's true. We did this because intrusive thoughts and negative beliefs are common symptoms of PTSD and are symptoms that can be particularly difficult to deal with, because they are persistent and often pop up unexpectedly. By introducing you to all of these different skills, you will have a wider range of strategies available the next time you are struggling with distressing thoughts, memories, and beliefs. It's likely that some of these skills will work better for you than others, and that is completely okay. All that matters is that you apply one or more of these skills when you are struggling with thoughts, memories, and beliefs, and that you find the ones that work best for you for certain thoughts and in certain situations. The more you do this, the more you will be able to break unhelpful patterns of thinking, reducing their influence on your behavior and life.

CHAPTER 5

Using Exposure to Overcome Avoidance and Gain Freedom

In this chapter, we focus on one of the most helpful sets of skills that you can use to manage your PTSD symptoms—exposure. Exposure therapy involves purposely entering into experiences that you fear in a structured, safe, and systematic way. Across many studies, researchers have discovered that exposure therapy is a powerful and effective treatment for PTSD as well as several anxiety disorders, such as obsessive-compulsive disorder, social anxiety disorder, and others (Olatunji, Cisler, and Deacon 2010). In fact, exposure is an important part of the most effective treatments for PTSD: prolonged exposure (Olatunji, Cisler, and Deacon 2010) and cognitive processing therapy (Resick, Monson, and Chard 2008). Even if you're not in a treatment that involves exposure, you can still benefit from strategies and skills based on this type of treatment. That's what we focus on in this chapter: how to use exposure to increase tolerance of what's going on inside you, reduce PTSD symptoms, help you move toward important goals, and improve and broaden your life.

To many people with PTSD, the word *exposure* sounds frightening. Why would someone want to approach something as painful as the emotions and thoughts that accompany PTSD? Well, we would imagine that even when you don't approach your PTSD symptoms, they are still present and affecting your life. And as we mentioned in chapter 1, avoiding your symptoms can make your problems worse. Exposure is, in many ways, the opposite of avoidance, and it's one of the best ways to overcome it. It can help you reduce your symptoms and increase your freedom to engage in activities that are important to you. Before we talk more about exposure, we will revisit our discussion of the problems with avoidance from chapter 1.

Problems with Avoidance

Avoidance is one of your worst enemies in your efforts to overcome PTSD. We believe that avoidance of internal experiences (such as thoughts, sensations, emotions, and flashbacks) and external situations (people, places, and events) related to trauma keeps your symptoms of PTSD alive. Avoidance is the fuel that drives PTSD. We think this happens for a couple of reasons:

- By avoiding situations (or emotions, thoughts, or memories) that you fear, you never get the opportunity to learn that these situations are not as dangerous as your mind tells you they are. As a result, you will stay afraid or even become more afraid.

- Avoidance leads to other problems, such as limiting your activities, making your life smaller and smaller, and reducing your opportunity to do things that are important to you. It is no surprise that many people with PTSD also struggle with depression. Having a full and meaningful life, including pleasurable activities, time with other people, social support, rewarding or meaningful occupational activities (volunteer work or jobs), and so on, can help you recover and maintain your recovery from PTSD. Avoidance deprives you of this opportunity.

How Fear and Avoidance Can Spread Across Your Life

Fear and avoidance can also spread to many other areas of your life. As we've discussed, when you first experience a traumatic event, it's natural to be afraid of things related to the trauma, such as people, places, feelings, thoughts, or sensations. Over time, however, instead of just being afraid of the man who assaulted you, you might start to become afraid of all men, or all men with particular characteristics (height, hair color, and so on). Instead of being afraid of being out in the open in a combat situation, you might become afraid of being out in the open even in a regular place, where any kind of danger is unlikely (such as a park). We call this *generalization*.

These situations are neither traumatic nor dangerous (or at least, no more dangerous than other activities of daily living). You probably know this intellectually. Nevertheless, you are still afraid of these situations. They have become connected to the danger you experienced during the traumatic event.

The same goes for feelings and memories. Many people who have experienced traumatic events feel afraid and uncomfortable with the memories and thoughts related to the trauma. Now, we know that memories and thoughts can't actually do you any harm (even though they can be emotionally painful); the actual traumatic event was harmful, not the memory or thought of it. Nevertheless, thoughts and memories can also seem dangerous. And what do we tend to do when something seems dangerous? We avoid it, and if we can't avoid it, we escape it. This is perfectly natural and understandable. Why would you want to spend time in a terrifying place or with people who frighten you? If your thoughts, feelings, or memories seem dangerous, why wouldn't you want to avoid or escape them at all costs? And yet, at the same time, avoiding or escaping people, situations, memories, thoughts, and feelings related to your trauma can hinder your recovery.

Here's how it works: the more you avoid, the more you confirm the idea that what you're afraid of is dangerous and should be avoided. Let's say, for example, that you really want to get out into your garden and plant flowers, but you are afraid of garter snakes. Now, you may know that garter snakes are not particularly dangerous. They rarely bite, and they're nonvenomous. So even if they do bite, you won't be harmed. Nevertheless, you feel afraid and avoid the garden. The garden starts to seem like a scary place, because it's associated with garter snakes, which are associated with danger. And the more you avoid the garden, the more you confirm the idea that it is a place that should be avoided. People keep telling you it's perfectly safe to get out there in the dirt, and you already know this. You "know" intellectually that you're not really in danger in your garden. Nevertheless, you still avoid the garden, because your emotions and thoughts tell you that it is dangerous.

What do you think you need to do to overcome your fear? You need to do the opposite of what you might feel like doing—get out and spend a lot of time in the garden. Even better, you need to look for and spend time with the garter snakes. That way, your brain will learn through experience that not only is the garden safe but so are garter snakes. As you experience the garden and all that it entails as safe, those thoughts and feelings that can drive avoidance will start to subside. This will make it easier to garden anytime you want.

Exposure Is a Way to Become Free

Getting out in the garden is what we mean by *exposure*. Exposure involves purposely putting yourself in contact with things that you are afraid of. If you're afraid of walking down the street, exposure involves repeatedly walking down the street. If you're afraid of going out alone to a park, exposure involves getting yourself out to that park on your own, repeatedly. If you're afraid of memories of your traumatic event, exposure involves purposely remembering the traumatic event—getting in contact with your memories. Indeed, the best way to overcome fear is to face the very thing you're afraid of. In table 5.1, we have included a brief summary of the three main ways to use exposure to become free.

Table 5.1. Three Primary Types of Exposure

In Vivo Interoceptive Exposure	This type of exposure involves purposely exposing yourself to people, places, objects, or events that you tend to fear or avoid. *In vivo exposure* means exposure in real life. If you're afraid of being outside in an open place, then in vivo exposure involves purposely going into open places. If you're afraid of being alone, in vivo exposure would involve purposely being alone. This type of exposure is designed to help you learn that the situations you fear are not particularly dangerous and that you can tolerate feelings of anxiety and fear.
Interoceptive Exposure	This type of exposure involves experiencing bodily sensations that you might be afraid of. You either pay mindful attention to these bodily sensations as they arise naturally, or you might do things purposely to make yourself feel certain sensations. For example, if you are afraid of having a strong heartbeat, you might run or do some vigorous physical activity. If you have a hard time with dizziness, you might spin around until you feel dizzy and allow yourself to experience that sensation. This type of exposure is designed to help you learn that physical sensations are not dangerous and that you can tolerate these sensations.
Imaginal Exposure	This type of exposure involves using your imagination to encounter things you tend to fear or avoid. The most common and effective type of imaginal exposure for PTSD is called *prolonged exposure*, which involves purposely remembering your traumatic event as if it were happening right now. Typically, you describe the event to your therapist in a lot of detail in the present tense ("Now I am merging onto the highway. A large white delivery truck is right ahead of me."). You record your descriptions and listen to them between therapy sessions. This type of exposure is designed to help you become less afraid of memories and thoughts related to your traumatic event.

At this point, you might be thinking it's time to stop reading this chapter. It's easy for us to say "face your fears and you'll overcome them." It's another thing altogether to actually do it. And there's no doubt that exposure is difficult work—perhaps the most difficult work you'll ever do. It's also one of the most effective and powerful ways to take your life back. And remember, you are in charge when it comes to exposure. Even though it may bring up some painful thoughts and emotions, you are always in control. So let's get started.

Getting Started: In Vivo Exposure

As described above in table 5.1, one type of exposure involves encountering real-life situations that you have been avoiding or that you are afraid of. This is called *in vivo exposure*. You can also think of this as *real-life* exposure (the Latin phrase *in vivo* means "in the living"). Over time, you will learn that many of the situations you're afraid of are actually safe. You might notice that your fear and anxiety go down. More importantly, you might feel a greater sense of freedom to do what's important to you.

List Your Feared or Avoided Activities

Start by listing activities or situations that you have been avoiding due to your PTSD. If you've gotten used to avoiding things, it can be hard to notice all of them. You might consider getting suggestions and feedback from a trusted friend, loved one, support person, or therapist. Whether you have help from a support person or not, you will have to be really honest with yourself as you come up with your list.

One way to start is to think back to the time before your PTSD symptoms began. Consider the types of activities you did back then, and ask yourself whether you have stopped doing some of those things. This may be challenging if your PTSD began long ago. If you have difficulty coming up with activities that you did before PTSD, think of things that you would like to be doing but are afraid of. You can also revisit exercise 2.5 in chapter 2 in which you identified your triggers for your PTSD symptoms. This may remind you of the types of situations or things that you avoid because they bring up PTSD symptoms.

Using exercise 5.1 below, make a note of these activities or situations. Try to organize this list so that the situations that you are least afraid of are at the bottom, and the ones you are most afraid of are at the top of the list. The second column is entitled "SUDS," which means "subjective units of distress scale"—the level of distress or fear that you experienced. Normally, this is rated on a scale from 0 (no distress) to 100 (the most distress you've ever experienced). In the column entitled "Avoidance," rate how much you avoid these situations, using a scale from 0 (I never avoid this situation) to 10 (I always avoid this situation). In the column entitled "Goal," please write down your goal for this activity. Exposure is likely to work best if you can connect what you're doing to goals that are important to you. Think of why it's important to you to do the activity, and specify exactly what you'd like to work toward. For instance, in the example of going for a walk alone, you can see that the goal is to walk three times a week for fitness. Finally, also in the Goal column, note how important this activity is for you, again on a scale of 0 to 10, with 10 being the most important.

Exercise 5.1. List Your Feared or Avoided Situations

Situation	SUDS	Avoidance	Goal
Initiating sexual activity with my partner	75	7	I would like to initiate sex more often. Importance = 8/10
Going out for a walk alone	85	9	I would like to go for a walk 3 times per week for fitness. Importance = 7

Schedule In Vivo Exposure Daily

Once you have a list of avoided situations, the next step is to schedule times to purposely enter these situations on a daily basis. Exposure works best if it is consistent, structured, and scheduled, especially at first. This will ensure that exposure becomes a habit that can compete with your old habit of avoiding. Most people are more likely to do something like exposure if they have it in their schedule. Don't wait until you feel like entering situations you're afraid of. When are you going to feel like doing that? Start with a plan, and take action based on your plan, not based on your mood or on how motivated you feel. Motivation often follows action, as opposed to the reverse. We also suggest that you practice exposure daily. Most of the scientific evidence for exposure is based on regular, daily practice. Your brain has well-worn pathways telling you that certain situations are dangerous. You've walked down those paths many times, to the point where the paths are easy, bramble-free, and clear. Exposure is like forging a new path. You have to get out there, clear the brush, and make sure the weeds and grass don't grow back. To do that, you have to work hard every day until you have a clear path. Know, however, that as you do this work, it is going to become easier and easier to resist taking the old path.

Keeping these points in mind, come up with a schedule of in vivo exposure activities. Start with items lower on your list—the easier ones. If you are seeing a therapist and getting help with this, you and your therapist might decide to start with items higher on the list. If you're doing this on your own, however, we recommend that you start with the items that you can best handle. We want you to have a successful experience with exposure. No matter what you choose to do, this is going to be hard work. You're probably going to feel more empowered and successful if you choose situations off the bat that you can stay in for long enough to learn something new.

Use exercise 5.2 below, the Daily Goal Worksheet for In Vivo Exposure, to keep track of your exposure goals, whether you achieved them, and how you felt during the exposures. Under "Day," simply write the day of the week on which you are scheduling your exposure practice. Under "Goal," write what your goal is. Choose something from your list (exercise 5.1) that you think you can manage. Write this down as your goal for that day. Under "Accomplished?" write yes or no, depending on whether you did or did not do the activity. If you did a different activity instead, write that in this column. If you didn't accomplish an activity, try to identify what barriers you encountered. Maybe you woke up late that day, or maybe you were experiencing intense, unpleasant thoughts and emotions that got the best of you. Write this down in the "Comments" section. It is important to be aware of barriers to doing exposure. The more you are aware of these barriers, the better able you will be to work around them during future exposures. Under "Max. SUDS," write the SUDS score for the highest level of distress you felt during the activity. This maximum SUDS could have occurred at the beginning, middle, or end of the activity. It doesn't matter when you felt the maximum SUDS—just write it in. Under "Min. SUDS," note the lowest level of SUDS you felt during the activity.

In the column entitled "Tolerance," note how much you believe you could tolerate being in that situation again in the future, using a scale from 0 (I could tolerate it for zero seconds) to 10 (I could tolerate it for ten hours). This last column is important. While we believe that you will notice your SUDS falling over time, this doesn't always happen, or it might not happen as soon as you'd like. Even if your SUDS remains moderate or high, however, you might still notice that you feel more and more able to tolerate being in the situation and to tolerate how you feel in the situation (such as afraid or anxious). The more you can tolerate frightening situations, the more freedom you will have to decide what to do and when to do it. Even if your fear is still present, it doesn't have to stop you from doing things that are important to you.

Finally, under "Comments," describe your experience in the exposure situation. Comment on how you felt and what the experience was like for you. Try to provide a balanced description of the situation, including both scary parts and less scary or even enjoyable parts. Comment on whether anything bad actually happened. If you felt proud of yourself for doing the activity, write that here. Give yourself some credit! This is really hard work. Writing these comments will help you learn the most from each exposure. Later on, when you feel some trepidation about entering one of the situations you've worked on, you can look back at your earlier comments to see what the experience was actually like.

Exercise 5.2. Daily Goal Worksheet for In Vivo Exposure

Day	Goal	Accomplished?	Max. SUDS	Min. SUDS	Tolerance
Monday	*Go for 15-min walk at 10 a.m.*	*Yes!*	*75*	*30*	*7*
Comments	*At first, my heart was pounding, and I didn't want to go. But I went anyway and walked for about fifteen minutes. I started off feeling really afraid (7.5/10), and it went up and down while I walked, but by the end, it was about 3/10. I tolerated my feelings pretty well. At one point, I jumped when I heard a sound in the bushes, but it was just a squirrel. Nothing bad happened. I actually kind of enjoyed it.*			

Day	Goal	Accomplished?	Max. SUDS	Min. SUDS	Tolerance
Tuesday					
Comments					
Wednesday					
Comments					
Thursday					
Comments					
Friday					
Comments					

Day	Goal	Accomplished?	Max. SUDS	Min. SUDS	Tolerance
Saturday					
Comments					
Sunday					
Comments					

You can download additional copies of the worksheet at http://www.newharbinger.com/32240. As you continue to practice in vivo exposure, there are a few key tips to keep in mind:

- *Exposure works best if you enter scary situations with your full awareness.* In other words, be mindful of your experiences. If you're afraid of going to a party, for example, make sure you're paying a lot of attention to the experience of being at the party. Observe and notice the people around you, how you feel, and the thoughts going through your mind.

- *Exposure works best if you avoid avoiding.* The exposure exercise of going to a party will be most effective if you avoid staying in the restroom the whole time, standing in the corner without talking to people, or hovering around the food tray. Jump into the situation with both feet, keeping your mind awake and staying in the situation. Don't let yourself escape or avoid, either physically (such as going to another room or hiding) or mentally (such as by distracting yourself, dissociating, pretending you're not there, using your smartphone, and so on).

- *Exposure works best if you stay in the situation long enough for your brain to learn something new.* People used to think that you should stay in a frightening situation until your SUDS rating goes down by about 50 percent. You could certainly still do that. If you do, you might learn that your anxiety and fear don't last forever. In fact, like waves on the ocean, they rise and fall. It's not really necessary, however, to stay until your fear level is cut in half. It's more important to stay in the situation until you actually learn something new. Hopefully, the main thing that you will learn is that the situations you expose yourself to are not harmful or threatening to your life or well-being. Another thing that you will learn is that you can tolerate the fear and anxiety that arise when you're in this situation— without having to avoid or escape them. Keep these two learning points in mind: first, the situations you're afraid of are not dangerous; and second, you can handle anxiety and fear.

- *Watch out for judgmental or worry thoughts.* When you initially enter a situation you are afraid of, your body will likely sound the alarm. This means that, in addition to some unpleasant emotions, you are likely going to experience some unpleasant thoughts. These thoughts may look like worries (*What if something bad happens when I do this?*) and doubts (*My anxiety is never going to go down. This isn't going to work.*). These thoughts are just a symptom of your body's fight-flight-or-freeze response. Be careful to not buy into them. If you notice that they are particularly strong, you may want to try some of the mindfulness exercises focused on thoughts in chapters 2 and 3. If you struggle with an exposure exercise, you also want to be careful to not buy into judgmental thoughts, such as *I am a failure* or *I am weak*. These thoughts are only going to activate shame, which is going to make it harder to do the exposure the next time. Be compassionate with yourself. Remember, this is hard work. If you find that a particular exposure exercise is difficult to complete, try to break it down into smaller goals. For example, if you struggle going to the park, you may first want to try sitting across the street from the park and then just sitting by the entrance of the park and so on. By breaking difficult situations into smaller goals, you will ultimately be able to address the larger goal.

- *Be aware of safety behaviors.* A *safety behavior* is any behavior or act that you engage in that makes it easier to approach a feared situation or activity. For example, taking an antianxiety medication before you go into a crowded store or having your cell phone available in case you experience a panic attack. Safety behaviors come in many different forms. So as you go through these exposure exercises, it is important to take a look at what you do during an exposure that provides you with some reassurance, comfort, or peace of mind. You may wonder why we are cautioning you about safety behaviors. As we said earlier, exposure works best when you stay in the situation long enough to learn something new. We want you to learn that you can tolerate fear and anxiety. We want you to learn that certain situations are not dangerous. If you engage in a safety behavior during an exposure, you may attribute any success you have to the safety behavior instead of to your own ability to approach a feared situation. This means that the connection between fear and the situation remains, and eventually, you may become highly reliant on the safety behavior. Safety behaviors, however, are not always bad. If you have a hard time starting exposure without safety behaviors, that's okay. Sometimes, a safety behavior can give you a greater sense of security and comfort that allows you to take part in an exposure exercise. If you take this approach, however, we recommend that you come up with a plan to give up the safety behavior at a later date. You can even do this in tiny increments. Once you practice exposure several times without the safety behavior, you will most likely find that you no longer feel the need for it.

- *Take reasonable precautions.* Even though we're recommending that you avoid safety behaviors, we are not recommending that you disregard safety entirely. Let's say you're afraid of walking down your street at night. Well, there's always a small chance that something could happen to you, depending on a number of factors, including where you live. Exposure doesn't involve naïvely placing yourself in harm's way. If there's a chance that you might not be safe, take precautions. Bring pepper spray, avoid walking down the street with headphones on, and remain aware of your surroundings. If you know any self-defense strategies, be ready to use them if you need to. In all likelihood, you will be perfectly safe, but it's important to take steps to ensure that's true.

Interoceptive Exposure

As we discussed earlier in this book, people with PTSD experience strong physical reactions, such as increased heart rate and emotions when confronted with a reminder of their traumatic event. When bodily sensations and emotions become strong or unpleasant, there is a good chance that you're going to want to avoid or escape them. You might try to avoid what reminded you of the traumatic event (the cue that might have triggered your bodily sensations), or you might try to avoid the sensations themselves. Normally, when something is dangerous, we can avoid it and feel safer. The problem with emotions and bodily sensations, however, is that it is difficult to avoid them: to completely avoid what your body is feeling, you would basically have to be out of your own body. Because of this, as we have discussed, *dissociation* is one of the coping strategies that you might've developed along with PTSD. Furthermore, avoidance and escape can keep these sensations stuck on high. Therefore, one way to facilitate in vivo exposure is to practice another kind of exposure that is designed to increase your tolerance for bodily sensations—*interoceptive exposure.*

As described in table 5.1, interoceptive exposure is the exposure to bodily sensations. Research has shown that it can help people with PTSD increase their tolerance for bodily sensations related to PTSD. Studies also have shown that interoceptive exposure can help them effectively complete other exposure exercises (Wald and Taylor 2007; Wald et al. 2010).

We would like to remind you here of two of the important points we made above, as both of these points apply to interoceptive exposure. First, keep your mind open so that you learn through your experience that your emotions and bodily sensations are not actually dangerous or harmful to you. Second, make sure you avoid avoiding or escaping. If you avoid or escape your emotions or bodily sensations, you won't give yourself a chance to learn that you can experience them safely. Further, if you avoid or escape, you won't get the chance to learn that you can actually tolerate your emotions and bodily sensations.

Practicing Interoceptive Exposure

There are many ways to practice interoceptive exposure. The first step is to figure out which bodily sensations you have a hard time with. Different people have trouble with different types of sensations. For some, it's shortness of breath; for others, a rapid or pounding heartbeat. Some people have a particularly hard time with sensations of heat or perspiration, with dizziness, or with a feeling of depersonalization (like you're not connected to yourself, or your thoughts and feelings seem unreal), and so on. On the list below, circle the sensations that you have the hardest time with. Now, before you do this, it's important to realize that you might not especially *like* any of these sensations. That's normal. We would like you to circle the ones that you are actually afraid of, that you have a tremendously hard time tolerating, or that are related to your PTSD.

- shortness of breath

- lightheadedness

- feelings of dizziness

- panting, breathing heavily

- pounding heart, rapid heartbeat

- feeling hot in various parts of your body

- perspiration

- tight muscles (such as in your chest, shoulders)

- a feeling of unreality (depersonalization)

- other _____

- other _____

Now that you've circled the ones you have a hard time with, you can probably guess what we're going to suggest next. Interoceptive exposure involves purposely experiencing sensations that you fear or avoid. So the next step is to purposely find a way to make these sensations happen, and ride them out for as long as you can. We've included a list below of ways to make certain sensations happen.

- Ways to induce *shortness of breath* include breathing really rapidly (purposely hyperventilating) or breathing through a straw. Don't do this for too long, or you may actually pass out, but try it for a few minutes, then repeat.

- You can induce *lightheadedness* by sitting in a chair with your head between your knees and then getting up really quickly.

- You can bring on feelings of *dizziness* by spinning in one spot (we recommend that you do this in a safe place with a carpeted floor or on your knees rather than standing), or by spinning around in a chair.

- To induce *panting, heavy breathing,* or a *rapid or pounding heartbeat,* you can briefly engage in intense exercise, such as running in place, doing jumping jacks, doing push-ups or lunges, walking quickly up a flight of stairs, or whatever gets your heart pounding and increases your respiration.

- You can make yourself feel *sensations of heat* using intense exercise, by wearing warm clothing and turning up the heat, sitting in a sauna or steam room, using an electric blanket, or tensing all of the muscles in your body repeatedly.

- *Perspiration* can be brought on by some of the strategies for inducing heat or heavy breathing.

- To give yourself a feeling of *tight muscles,* purposely tense the muscles in various places in your body. You could also notice the sensations as you lift weights.

- You can bring on a feeling of *unreality* (*depersonalization*) by staring at your own face in the mirror. It sounds like an odd thing to do, but after a while, many people notice a strange sensation that they are not the person they're looking at.

After you have circled the sensations to work on and decided which exercises to use to induce these feelings, schedule interoceptive exposure sessions for yourself. Use exercise 5.3 below to keep track of what you planned to do, whether you did it, your SUDS ratings, and your tolerance ratings. Also provide comments about your experiences, as you did above for your in vivo exposure practice.

Exercise 5.3. Interoceptive Exposure Worksheet

Day	Goal	Accomplished?	Max. SUDS	Min. SUDS	Tolerance
Monday	Spin in a chair for five minutes	Yes!	80	45	6
Comments	At first, I felt really scared and kind of sick. As the room was spinning around me, I felt out of control. I stopped spinning and paid attention to how I felt. The dizziness was rough, but I noticed that I wasn't in any kind of danger. I tried it again a few times, until it was about five minutes. It got easier the last couple of times. By the end, my SUDS was around 45, and I felt like I could mostly tolerate it (6/10), but I think I need to work on this one some more.				
Tuesday	Ride out intense anxiety	Yes!	85	55	7
Comments	I was just getting ready for work, and I got this huge rush of anxiety. I felt an adrenaline surge in my chest, my heart was pounding, and my whole body felt hot. I sat there and tried to ride it out by just focusing on how my body felt. It got really intense for a few minutes (SUDS = 85), and I felt like I was going to explode. But then the adrenaline surge went away, and my heart seemed to calm down. I was still a little sweaty, but I had cooled down to about SUDS = 55 in about ten minutes. I learned that I could tolerate these feelings without having to take medication or do anything to get rid of them.				
Wednesday					
Comments					

Day	Goal	Accomplished?	Max. SUDS	Min. SUDS	Tolerance
Thursday					
Comments					
Friday					
Comments					
Saturday					
Comments					
Sunday					
Comments					

As you did with the in vivo exposure exercises above, use exercise 5.3 to schedule yourself to do this exercise and to keep track of your experiences. (Additional copies of the worksheet are available at http://www.newharbinger.com/32240.)

Continue to practice this exercise when you experience mildly distressing emotions. After some time and practice, you will be ready to start using this exercise to get some experience with exposure to more distressing emotions—perhaps those emotions that are related directly to your traumatic experiences or PTSD. As mentioned above, exposure has the best evidence for alleviating emotions such as fear and anxiety.

Practicing Mindful Exposure to Emotions

Another way to practice interoceptive exposure is to pay mindful attention to the sensations of your emotions. As discussed above, exposure and mindfulness go hand in hand. Exposure is a lot more likely to be effective if you are awake and mindful of your experiences. Try out the exercise described below.

Exercise 5.4. Mindful Exposure to Emotions

1. Sit in a comfortable position with your feet flat on the floor and your back relatively straight and upright. Sitting in this way will help you remain alert throughout the exercise.

2. Next, focus on your breathing. Notice what it feels like to breathe in and breathe out. Notice which parts of your body move as you breathe in and out.

3. Think about a recent time when you felt fear or anxiety at a moderate level of intensity. Try to focus on a time when your fear or anxiety was about 4 or 5 on a scale from 0 to 10, where 0 is no emotion and 10 is the most intense emotion possible. Focus on this experience and try to get a clear picture of it in your mind.

4. Bring your attention back to your body and notice where in your body you feel the emotion. Scan your body from head to toe, paying attention to any sensations in your head, neck, shoulders, back, chest, abdomen, arms, hands, legs, and feet. Spend about ten seconds on each area of your body, stepping back in your mind and just paying attention to and noticing these sensations.

5. Once you have finished scanning your body, bring your attention to the parts of your body where you feel fear or anxiety. Zero in on the sensations. Watch them rise and fall in your mind's eye as you would watch waves on the ocean.

6. Bring your attention to any thoughts that are present, focusing on just noticing these thoughts as thoughts, without attaching to them. If you find yourself getting caught up in your thoughts or judging yourself for having them, notice that and then bring your attention back to just noticing the thoughts that are present.

7. See if you can bring your attention to any urges or desires you have to avoid or escape your experiences. Simply notice these urges or desires as they rise and fall, bringing attention to the way they change or stay the same. Avoid acting on them.

8. Keep focusing on the different experiences of your emotion without escaping or avoiding them. Continue to just notice your sensations, thoughts, and urges or desires without trying to push them away or change them. Do this for about ten to fifteen minutes, until the emotion subsides or until you feel like you can tolerate your experiences.

Imaginal Exposure

A third and very important type of exposure is called *imaginal exposure*, which involves exposing yourself to situations in your imagination. This type of exposure can be a good substitute for in vivo exposure when it is hard to find or get into the real-life situations that you're afraid of. Imaginal exposure can also be helpful when situations you're afraid of are not particularly safe. If, for example, you were afraid of walking in the dark alone, and you live in a dangerous neighborhood, you might opt to do imaginal exposure, imagining yourself in that situation, rather than walking around in the dark in your neighborhood.

Perhaps the most important type of imaginal exposure for PTSD is called *prolonged exposure*, which involves purposely reexperiencing a traumatic event in your imagination—bringing up the memory of the trauma in vivid detail and experiencing it as if it's happening right now. This is probably the most difficult kind of work that anyone with PTSD can do. The last thing you probably want to do is to relive the traumatic event, even just in your memory. You probably would prefer it if the memory were to disappear entirely. So, why do this? Well, one good reason is that it works. There's lots of evidence that treatments including prolonged exposure are very effective for PTSD (Olatunji, Cisler, and Deacon 2010). After going through prolonged exposure, many people report that many of their symptoms have improved considerably. Prolonged exposure can also help you learn that the memories of your traumatic event are not dangerous. The traumatic event itself may have been damaging, but the memories of it can't harm you. These memories will never be pleasant, but they are not dangerous. Prolonged exposure can take the power out of your traumatic memories, reduce your PTSD symptoms, and help you move forward in your life.

Even though prolonged exposure can be such an effective treatment, we're not going to walk you through exercises for it in this book, because prolonged exposure is best done with a therapist who can help guide you through the exercises, discuss your reactions with you, help you remain safe, and support you in this difficult work. We don't recommend that you do prolonged exposure alone. If you're interested in figuring out where you can find a therapist who does prolonged exposure, you might consider looking up your state or provincial psychological association to see if they have a referral list or service. The final chapter in this book also offers some websites that can help you find prolonged-exposure providers. If you are a veteran, you can often receive this type of treatment through your country's veteran services. Prolonged exposure is a highly specialized treatment requiring expertise, so be sure to ask any provider about her or his experience with prolonged exposure. Finally, the American Psychological Association's Division 12 (Society of Clinical Psychology) has a helpful resource page on prolonged exposure that you might be interested in visiting: http://www.div12.org/psychological -treatments/disorders/post-traumatic-stress-disorder/prolonged-exposure-therapy.

Boosting the Effects of Exposure

There are a few ways to get the most out of the exposure exercises we've described above. First, exposure works best when you do it repeatedly. If you start off trying the exercises out just a couple of days per week, try to work up to every day or even more than once per day. Try to do both an in vivo exposure exercise and a mindful exposure to emotions exercise at least once per day.

Second, exposure works best when you do it in a variety of different situations. Let's say you're afraid of going for a walk, and you learn that you can tolerate walking down your own street. That would be excellent, but what about other streets in other places or neighborhoods? To truly become free of the fear, you will probably have to broaden your horizons and try to walk down many different streets in many different places, under different conditions (daytime, dusk, evening, and so on). The same goes for bodily sensations. Try to practice interoceptive exposure to a variety of bodily sensations.

Third, you can boost the effects of exposure by taking it up a notch. Let's say you're afraid of walking alone outside, and you're already out for a walk. Well, you could take it up a notch by deciding to go to a coffee shop until it gets darker so that you have to walk home in the dark. Or, if you're walking with a friend, say goodbye to your friend and walk home alone. If you're afraid of attending a meeting with other people, consider actually speaking or expressing an opinion during the meeting (assuming you're also afraid of speaking in front of people). Taking it up a notch means that you look for ways to amp up the fear or anxiety in the middle of your exposures. This might seem counterproductive, but some research has suggested that making the situation more stressful while you're in the middle of it can make exposure even more effective (Craske et al. 2014).

Maintain Your Gains by Reminding Yourself of What You've Learned

If you want to maintain what you've gained through exposure, one important thing to remember is that exposure is designed to help you learn something new. You're basically learning that situations you perceive as dangerous or threatening are actually safe. You're also learning that you can tolerate the experiences that come up (the fear, anxiety, and uncomfortable sensations) in these situations. Exposure is all about learning. The trick is to remember what you've learned. We've all learned a ton of things that we don't seem to remember later on without appropriate reminders. Therefore, when it comes to exposure, we highly recommend that you take steps to remind yourself of what you've learned. Below are a few ways to do this. Consider other ways that might work for you.

- Save the worksheets from this chapter or put them in a scrapbook, and come back to them. Read through and try to remember your experiences during exposure practices. Remind yourself of what you've learned.

- Set a reminder or alert on your phone to go off when you're going to be in a feared or anxiety-provoking situation. Perhaps the reminder could say something like, "I've done this before, nothing bad happened, and I could handle my feelings."

- Incorporate a sound (like a particular type of beep, tone, or song) into the very end of your exposure exercises. Then play this sound to yourself when you enter other similar situations. Soon the sound might become linked to how you have felt and what you have learned during exposure. You could also do this with a particular word. For example, when people practice muscle relaxation, they sometimes say the word *relax* to themselves right when they relax their muscles. Over time, the word itself begins to trigger feelings of relaxation.

Moving Forward

Okay, so we've taken you through some ways to get started with exposure. Exposure is one of the most powerful treatments we have for PTSD and related problems. While we recommend that you see a therapist to help walk you through exposure, you can get a good start on your own as well. Remember the pitfalls of avoidance: it prevents you from learning that what you're afraid of isn't dangerous, and it can stop you from building the life you want to live. Exposure is a way to become free to do what's important to you and to feel your own emotions without having to avoid or escape them. There are many different types of exposure, but we focused on two specific types in this chapter: in vivo exposure and interoceptive exposure. If you practice these powerful strategies on a regular basis, we are confident that you will be able to start taking your life back from PTSD. Also, remember to consider our suggestions on how to boost the effects of exposure and on how to remember what you've learned about yourself.

CHAPTER 6

Skills for Regulating Intense Emotions

Although problems with anxiety are at the core of PTSD, people with PTSD actually struggle with a number of intense emotions that can be difficult to regulate, such as guilt, sadness, and anger. The arousal that goes along with PTSD can make all emotions more intense—and this intensity can be more difficult to regulate. It takes more effort to regulate intense emotions. If you have PTSD, you've probably noticed that there are times when your emotions feel very overwhelming and you aren't sure how to manage them. The good news is that there are a number of skills for regulating emotions that can help. Some of these skills are helpful for intense emotions in general, and others are more useful for specific emotions. This chapter will cover both sets of skills. We'll begin with the skills for regulating emotions in general: from experiencing and understanding your emotions to taking a step back from your emotions and focusing your attention on something else. Then we'll describe some specific skills for managing two of the most difficult emotions that often go along with PTSD: anger and shame.

Approaching and Experiencing Emotions

One of the best ways to regulate emotions is to allow yourself to experience them. If your emotions often feel intense and overwhelming, this probably seems counterintuitive. You may be thinking, *Wouldn't getting in touch with my emotions make them even more overwhelming?* As surprising as this may be, the answer to that question is no. Many people think that avoiding their emotions is the best strategy for managing emotions, but this can actually make them feel even more overwhelming. In fact, research shows that trying to avoid emotions can increase the intensity and frequency of those emotions (Hayes, Strosahl, and Wilson 2011).

On the contrary, experiencing an emotion and letting it run its course allows that emotion to pass. Allowing yourself to experience your emotions will make them last for a shorter amount of time than trying to get rid of them. So how do you go about allowing yourself to experience your emotions? The first step is to resist the urge to avoid your emotions. As difficult as this may be, the best way to combat avoidance is to notice the urge to avoid and then gently turn your attention toward your emotions. Whenever you notice an emotion coming on, focus on staying in the present moment and turning your attention toward that emotion. Use the mindfulness skills described in chapters 2 and 3 to help you observe and describe your emotion.

Begin by noticing the thoughts, bodily sensations, and action urges that go along with the emotion. If you find it easier to focus on the bodily sensations that accompany the emotion, start by bringing your attention to how the emotion feels in your body and describing all of the various physical sensations you are having. Then bring your attention to the thoughts you are having and the action urges you are experiencing. If you find yourself getting caught up in your thoughts, gently turn your attention back to one of the other components of the emotion. Also, remember to remain objective when describing your emotions. Don't judge your emotions or label them as "good" or "bad." Instead, simply describe each component of the emotion and your experience of it objectively, in a neutral, matter-of-fact way.

Next, as the emotion develops, notice how it changes and whether it becomes stronger or weaker. Do your thoughts or bodily sensations change as the emotion develops? Pay attention to all these experiences. Try to ride the wave of your emotion. Think of yourself as a surfer riding the waves in the ocean—only this time, the wave is your current emotion. Notice how the wave crests and breaks. And keep in mind that as uncomfortable as your emotions may be, they will not hurt you. They are just your body's way of trying to communicate with you. Remind yourself that most emotions peak fairly soon after you notice them and dissipate shortly afterward.

Finally, as your emotion begins to weaken, notice once again how your body feels. What thoughts are you having now? How quickly does the emotion decrease in intensity? How do you feel about the fact that you stayed present with your emotion and didn't try to avoid it? Try practicing this skill each time you feel an emotion, and you might be amazed by just how quickly your emotions will pass if you allow yourself to experience them.

Although mindfully observing your emotions is one helpful strategy for allowing yourself to experience your emotions, there are a number of other strategies you can also use to get in touch with your emotions. These strategies may be particularly useful if you have been avoiding your emotions for so long that you find it difficult to get in touch with them.

- *Write about your emotions.* Writing about how you're feeling and the bodily sensations, thoughts, and action urges you're experiencing in the moment can be a simple way of getting in touch with your emotions. Even if you aren't sure exactly what emotions you're experiencing, journaling about how you feel and what you notice can help you connect with them. Focusing on what you've written and reading your description of how you feel can also help you experience the emotions.

- *Express your feelings through artwork.* Sometimes people struggle to write about their feelings because they aren't sure how to describe them. If that's the case for you, consider drawing or painting a picture of how you are feeling. This will put you in touch with your emotions.

- *Listen to or play music.* Music can be a powerful strategy for connecting with your emotions. Just listening to music can put people in touch with a wide variety of emotions, such as sadness, fear, anger, or joy.

- *Talk about your feelings with others.* Telling someone how you feel is a helpful strategy for getting in touch with your emotions. In order to describe your feelings to someone else, you have to allow yourself to experience those emotions to some extent. And talking about your feelings to someone else can actually help you connect with those emotions even more.

Identifying Your Emotions

Once you've allowed yourself to experience your emotions, the next step is to label your emotions and identify how you are feeling. Having *emotional clarity*—knowing exactly what emotions you are feeling—can actually make your emotions seem more manageable. When you know how you're feeling, you're in a better position to figure out how to make yourself feel better. You might have already noticed that different coping strategies work better for different emotions. When you feel sad, you might find it comforting to talk to your best friend or to curl up in a hot bath with some soothing music. When you're angry, you might want to go for a long run or release energy in another way. The things that work to make you feel better when you're upset depend a lot on exactly what emotion you're feeling at the time. That's why it is important to learn to identify how you're feeling and to label your emotions.

All emotions are made up of three different components: cognitive (the thoughts that go through your mind), physical (the way your body responds), and behavioral (the things you do or have urges to do). Let's take anger as an example. The cognitive component of anger may include thoughts such as *This shouldn't be happening to me! What a jerk!* or *This is so unfair!* At a physical level, feelings of anger are often accompanied by a racing heart, clenched fists, tense muscles, or a tight jaw. And the behavioral component of anger may include urges to scream, throw things, or punch something or someone.

Even though all emotions are made up of these three different components, you might not always be aware of or in touch with each of these components. For instance, you might not know how you're feeling until you find yourself wanting to cry or scream. Or you might be aware of sad thoughts but feel completely out of touch with how sadness feels in your body. At other times, you might only be aware of your bodily sensations and have no clue what emotion you're experiencing. Therefore, one of the first steps in learning to identify your emotions is to become more aware of each of their components. The more aware you are of these components, the better able you'll be to identify exactly what emotion you're feeling. And knowing exactly how you are feeling is going to make it easier to figure out the best way to cope with those emotions. Table 6.1 provides some examples of the different components of several basic emotions. See if they match your experience. Then, the next time you experience one of these emotions, see if you can identify all of its components.

Table 6.1. Components of Different Emotions

Emotion	Bodily Sensations	Thoughts	Actions or Action Urges
Fear	Racing heart Sweating Muscle tension Tunnel vision Trembling Shortness of breath	*I am in danger.* *I am not safe.* *Something bad is about to happen.*	Freezing Running away Lashing out Hiding
Sadness	Tightness behind the eyes Sinking feeling in the pit of your stomach Slowed heart rate	*Nobody loves me.* *I am all alone.* *Things will never get better.*	Isolating Crying Seeking support Wanting a hug
Anger	Racing heart Shortness of breath Muscle tension Tightness in your jaw	*Everyone is against me.* *This is unfair.* *This isn't right.*	Raising your voice Screaming Throwing something Punching or hitting Asserting your needs Confronting someone

Now that you have a better understanding of the different components of emotions, you can use this information to help identify your emotions as you experience them. Use the worksheet from exercise 6.1 (available for download at http://www.newharbinger.com/32240) to monitor your emotions and their different components. Whenever you experience an emotion this week, fill out this worksheet. Begin by focusing your attention on your bodily sensations. Write down how your body feels and any sensations you notice. Focus on your heart rate, breathing, muscles, and posture, and write down everything you observe. Next, see if you can identify the thoughts associated with your emotion. What thoughts are running through your mind? Write down all the thoughts you notice. Then bring your attention to the action urges you're experiencing. What does this emotion make you want to do or say? How does it make you want to act? Focus on these urges, and write down everything you notice. Next, write down what you did in response to this emotion, both positive and negative. Did you act on your action urges or do something else? Write down any actions you took. Finally, take a step back and use the information in the first four columns to try to identify the emotion you're experiencing. Based on the answers you provided, see if you can figure out what you're feeling. Write this down in the last column.

Keep this monitoring form with you throughout your day, and fill them out whenever you notice that you're experiencing an emotion. By completing this form whenever you experience an emotion, you'll start to learn how different emotions feel in your body, how the thoughts that go along with one emotion differ from those that go along with another, and how different emotions make you want to act. Identifying the different components of your emotions and becoming more aware of each of them will make it easier to label your emotions and identify exactly how you're feeling.

Exercise 6.1. Emotion Monitoring Form

Bodily Sensations	Thoughts	Action Urges	Actions	Emotion

Identifying the Information Provided by Emotions

Once you've identified your emotions, see if you can identify the information provided by them. Remember that emotions are functional and serve a purpose. They provide important information about your environment. For this reason, it can be helpful to figure out why you're having an emotion and the information it's providing. Approach your emotions as a friend or helpful guide, rather than an enemy. Figure out why they're there and what they're telling you.

So what kinds of information do your emotions provide?

- Fear signals threat or danger.

- Anger tells you that something you need or want is being blocked in some way or that you've been violated in some way.

- Sadness signals loss.

- Guilt is a sign that you've done something that goes against your values.

- Happiness signals that you're in a situation that is rewarding and meaningful.

Identifying the information provided by your emotions and using that information to guide your behavior can help you respond more effectively. This will also allow your emotions to pass more quickly. Think of your emotions as someone knocking at your door. If you don't answer, that person is going to keep knocking at your door louder and louder until you respond. The same thing happens with emotions. If you don't listen to your emotions, they tend to grow in intensity until you have no choice but to attend to them. On the other hand, if you listen to your emotions, they are able to pass.

Use exercise 6.2 to identify the information provided by your emotions. Each time you identify or label an emotion, consider what it's telling you and how you can use that information to guide your behavior. First, briefly describe the situation that brought up the emotion. Next, list all of the emotions you experienced. Then, for each emotion you listed, use the third column to write down the information you think that emotion was providing you about the situation. Why did you experience this emotion? What was it telling you about the situation? Was it signaling danger or a threat of some kind (fear)? Were you experiencing a loss or a potential loss (sadness)? Were you doing something important to you (excitement) but concerned that it may not go well (anxiety)?

Next, in the fourth column, write down how you responded to that information. What did you do? Did you listen to the information provided by your emotion and respond accordingly? Or did you make another choice? Remember, just because an emotion is telling us to act in a certain way doesn't mean we have to obey. In fact, in some situations, it may be in our best interest to not act directly on the information being provided by an emotion. For example, if you get anxious during a meeting, it probably wouldn't be effective to run out of the room. The anxiety signals that the meeting is important to you, and that information can help you take it seriously and prepare in advance. However, responding to the signal of a threat by taking it literally and running away wouldn't be as helpful. Generally, it's most helpful to consider the information provided by your emotions and then assess how best to act on that information.

Finally, use the fifth column to identify if there were other ways you could have acted on the information provided by your emotions. Pay particular attention to responses that may have been more effective, or that would have used the information provided by your emotions in a more helpful way. We recommend that you keep several copies of this exercise with you so that you can fill them out throughout your day (they are available for download at http://www .newharbinger.com/32240). Filling them out as soon as you can after you have noticed and labeled an emotion will provide the best information, because it will be fresh in your mind.

Exercise 6.2. Identifying the Information Provided by Your Emotions

Situation	Emotion or Emotions	Information	Response	Other Response

Distraction Skills

So far, the skills in this chapter have focused on the benefits of experiencing and better understanding your emotions. And there is a lot of evidence that getting in touch with your emotions can help them pass and make them less overwhelming. Sometimes, however, when you are really upset, the best way to deal with your emotions is to focus your attention on something else. This will give your emotions time to run their course and lessen in intensity, which will make them easier to manage. In addition, distracting yourself from intense emotions can help you resist urges to act on those emotions in unhelpful ways or to avoid them in ways that you'll later regret. There are all kinds of distraction skills that you can use to refocus your attention. The key is simply finding something else to capture your attention.

Before we review these skills, however, it's important to keep in mind that you can overuse distraction. You might find that this works so well that you're always distracting yourself whenever you get upset. The problem with overusing distraction is that too much distraction can turn into avoidance, and by now you probably understand the problems that go along with too much avoidance. So we suggest that you use this skill in moderation—only to make it through a difficult time. Then, when your emotions have lessened in intensity or it is safe to experience them, stop distracting and turn your attention back toward your emotions. Using distraction skills in combination with some of the other skills we described above is the best recipe for success. Some of the most helpful distraction skills come from dialectical behavior therapy (Linehan 1993b, 2015). These are reviewed below.

Do Something

One of the best ways to distract yourself from an intense emotion is to throw yourself into an activity that will capture your attention (Linehan 1993b, 2015). Having something active to focus on is an excellent distraction. Another nice thing about this skill is that the possibilities are endless. You can choose almost any activity, as long as it is interesting, stimulating, or hard to ignore. As long as it captures your attention, it's sure to be helpful. Different activities that you may find helpful are described below.

- *Do something physically demanding.* One way to distract yourself from an intense emotion is to do something physically demanding, like aerobics, rock-climbing, hiking, or swimming. Throwing yourself into an activity that pushes your body and requires a lot of physical energy will help keep your attention focused on your body and the activity at hand. An added benefit of a physically demanding activity is that it will help burn off some of the energy that goes along with intense emotions.

- *Do an outdoor activity.* Many people find that doing something outdoors can be a better distraction than being indoors. When you're outdoors, surrounded by nature, there are all kinds of things that can capture your attention, from the temperature and feel of the air to the sounds you hear, the sights around you, and the things you smell. And the more senses that are captured by an activity, the more it will grab your attention. So if you need a distraction, go outside and do something. Take a walk and notice what you see, feel, hear, and smell. Rake your yard. Shovel some snow. Watch kids play. Try to identify the birds you see and hear. Do yard work. Observe the sights and sounds around you.

- *Do some work.* Throwing yourself into work can be a great distraction. Not only can it take your mind off your emotions, it has the benefit of helping you accomplish something. And getting something done that you need to get done can definitely help reduce your stress and make it easier to manage intense emotions. So find some chore or task that you need to do and focus all of your attention on just that. Do the laundry that has piled up. Clean your bathroom. Balance your checkbook. Mow your lawn. Work on your homework from school or therapy. It doesn't matter what you do, as long as you focus all of your attention on completing it.

- *Do something you enjoy.* Another helpful way to distract yourself from intense emotions is to do something you enjoy. The more you enjoy an activity, the more likely it is to capture your attention. So, do something you like! Get a meal at your favorite restaurant. Hang out with a good friend. Watch your favorite television show or movie. Engage in your favorite hobby. Go shopping or to a museum. As long as you choose something you really enjoy, you can't go wrong.

Get Your Mind Busy

One of the best ways to distract yourself is to give your mind something else to focus on (Linehan 1993b, 2015). Although throwing yourself into an activity can be a really helpful skill, it can sometimes be difficult to keep your mind from returning to whatever upset you. Just because your body is active doesn't mean that your mind will follow suit. Therefore, one way to distract yourself from an intense emotion is to give your mind something else to focus on. If you keep your mind busy, it won't have a chance to think about anything else. There are many ways to keep your mind busy. Some of our favorites are listed below.

- *Make your mind work.* If your mind is working hard, there won't be time for it to focus on your emotion. The key to this skill is to get your mind engaged in an activity that really requires focus. Do math equations in your head. Starting at zero, keep adding seven until you exceed one hundred; then begin subtracting seven until you reach zero again. Repeat this process. Do a crossword puzzle or word game. Play a challenging game on your phone. Play a stimulating computer game that really makes you think. Count the holes in the ceiling tiles. Count the number of clicks of a second hand on a clock. Try to come up with the name of an animal or a city that starts with each letter of the alphabet.

- *Use your imagination.* One way to keep your mind busy is to give it something really captivating and positive to focus on. Imagine your favorite vacation spot or the place you'd most like to visit. See if you can really picture yourself there. Imagine something you've always wanted to do and try to picture yourself doing it. Try to bring to mind all of the sights, sounds, smells, and other sensations you would experience in this situation. Imagine someone you are attracted to or a celebrity you'd like to spend time with.

Create Strong Sensations

Another way to distract yourself from your emotions is to create a sensation that is so powerful or strong that you can't help but focus on it (Linehan 1993b). The basic idea behind this skill is that really intense sensations can jolt you out of your head and capture your attention. At some point, it's just not possible to ignore intense sensations. Your attention is pulled to the sensation and, as a result, away from anything else. The other nice thing about this skill is that you can focus on any of your five senses, although we find that focusing on taste, smell, and touch tend to work best.

- *Taste.* Suck on a candy with a strong flavor, such as spicy cinnamon or sour lemon or citrus. Place a small amount of wasabi paste on your tongue and notice the feelings. Bite into a raw jalapeño pepper or suck on a lemon.

- *Smell.* When using this skill, look for smells that are really strong or potent. Some people find that unpleasant smells work better than pleasant ones for creating a strong sensation that is difficult to ignore. Slice an onion and breathe in the fumes. Buy some old-school scratch-and-sniff stickers and use some of the unpleasant smelling ones. Open a bottle of vinegar and breathe deeply. Light a bunch of scented candles with strong fragrances. Spray strongly scented perfume or cologne.

- *Touch.* Focus on sensations that are jarring and will capture your attention. Hold a piece of ice in your hand until it melts. Hold ice against your neck or forehead. Put a bunch of ice cubes in a plastic bag and hold onto them until you can't take it anymore. Take a cold shower. Sit in a cold bath. Take a shower, and turn the temperature back and forth from hot to cold. On a really cold day, run outside with light clothing on.

- *Hearing.* Listen to loud music that is upbeat or happy. Listen to your favorite song and sing along. Listen to music that gives you a jolt, such as heavy metal, if you're not used to it. Find sounds on your computer or the Internet and play them at a loud volume. Blow on a whistle.

- *Sight.* Focus your attention on an image that really captures your attention. Look at pictures with vibrant colors and strong lines. Look at artwork that you find compelling. Watch a video of something exciting or that you really enjoy. Focus your attention on every aspect of the image.

Now that you've learned all kinds of ways to focus your attention on something other than your emotion, it's time to put these skills into action. As we mentioned earlier, the key to distraction is to do something that captures your attention. Therefore, it's important to try out various activities and see just how captivating they are. Although what works best to distract you will probably depend on the situation, there are going to be some distraction skills that just seem to work better for you in general than others. Use exercise 6.3 to get a better understanding of the distraction activities that are best for you. This worksheet lists many of the skills we reviewed in this chapter to help distract yourself from your emotions. Filling out this worksheet will be a reminder to use these skills and will help you figure out which ones work the best for you. First, rate the intensity of your emotion on a scale from 0 (no emotion at all) to 10 (the most intense emotion ever) and put your rating in the "Emotion Before" column. Then try out some of the skills listed in the table. After you use each skill, immediately rate your emotion again on a scale from 0 to 10 in the "Emotion After" column. After you have done this a few times, you might notice that some strategies work better for you than others. Use the bottom of the worksheet to take notes on what you tried, what did or did not work for you, and what you might do the next time you want to distract yourself from an intense emotion.

Exercise 6.3. Skills for Distracting Yourself from Intense Emotions

Distraction Skill	Emotion Before (0–10)	Emotion After (0–10)
Do Something		
Do something physically demanding		
Do an outdoor activity		
Do some work		
Do something you enjoy		
Get Your Mind Busy		
Make your mind work		
Use your imagination		
Create Strong Sensations		
Taste		
Smell		
Touch		
Hearing		
Sight		
Comments		

Self-Soothing Skills

When people feel upset, it's common to want to be comforted in some way. Sometimes we seek comfort in people close to us. Although this can be a great way to manage emotions, loved ones may not always be available to support you when you really need help. They may not live close by, or you might need help at a time when they are not available, such as the middle of the night. Therefore, it is important to develop ways to comfort yourself. These skills are sometimes called *self-soothing skills.*

So how do you come up with self-soothing skills? Well, the first thing to do is to focus on your senses: touch, taste, smell, sight, and hearing. The best self-soothing skills are those that introduce comforting sensations to one or more of these five senses. Some of the sensations people find most soothing and comforting are described below (Linehan 1993b, 2015). Many of these were taken from our book, *The Dialectical Behavior Therapy Skills Workbook for Anxiety* (Chapman, Gratz, and Tull 2009).

- *Touch.* Introduce sensations that soothe your body. Put on clothing that has a soothing texture, like a fuzzy sweater, a flannel shirt, a soft cotton sweatshirt or T-shirt, a cozy fleece, or a silk shirt. Focus on the feeling of the fabric against your skin. Take a warm bubble bath or hot shower, or sit in a hot tub. Focus your attention on the feeling of the water against your skin. Sit in a sauna or relax in the sun, focusing on the warmth on your skin. Get a massage, or give yourself a massage! Pet your cat or dog (or another animal), focusing on the feel of the fur against your skin. Hug a friend or loved one. Wrap yourself up in a warm, fluffy blanket and curl up on a comfortable chair or in bed. Sit in front of a fire and focus on the warmth you feel.

- *Taste.* Eat your favorite comfort food, such as mashed potatoes, macaroni and cheese, cinnamon buns, sushi, or freshly baked bread. Sip a cup of hot cocoa or tea (or some other hot drink). On a hot day, eat a Popsicle or ice cream. Eat dark chocolate (this also releases feel-good chemicals). Eat a piece of fresh fruit and focus on the flavors.

- *Smell.* Burn incense or light a scented candle. Focus your attention on the scents that are released. Apply scented lotion to your skin and inhale the aroma. Go to a flower shop, botanical garden, or arboretum and smell the flowers. Inhale the aroma of lavender or vanilla. Go outside and breathe in fresh air. Bake cookies or bread. Smell fresh coffee beans or brew some fresh coffee. Cut some fresh herbs or open jars of spices and breathe in deeply. Light a fire and focus on the smell of the smoke and burning wood.

- *Sight.* Look at pictures of loved ones or a favorite vacation spot. Look at pictures that you find soothing or that relax you, like the beach, a sunset, or a beautiful mountain. Go to the beach and watch the waves hit the sand. Watch the sunset. Watch the clouds in the sky or leaves rustling in the breeze. Watch your pet or children play or sleep. Watch the flames of a fire or candle move and dance in the air.

- *Hearing.* Listen to relaxing music. Listen to birds sing. Listen to children playing. Take a walk through the woods or around your neighborhood and listen to the sounds of nature. Sit outside at dusk and listen to the crickets. Go to the beach and listen to the sound of waves crashing on the shore. Light a fire and listen to the pop and crackle of the wood.

As you practice these skills, make sure to focus your attention completely on your sensations. Stay in the moment. If you find yourself getting distracted, simply notice that and then turn your attention back to your senses.

Use the worksheet in exercise 6.4 to come up with some of your own self-soothing strategies. Anything you find comforting and nurturing will do the trick. Focus on each of your five senses and different things that you find most comforting. See if you can identify five different activities for each of your senses.

Exercise 6.4. Identifying Self-Soothing Strategies

Touch

- _____

- _____

- _____

- _____

- _____

- _____

Taste

- _____
- _____
- _____
- _____
- _____
- _____

Smell

- _____
- _____
- _____
- _____
- _____
- _____

Sight

- _____
- _____
- _____
- _____
- _____
- _____

Hearing

- _____
- _____
- _____
- _____
- _____
- _____

Now that you've identified some self-soothing strategies that may work for you, it's time to put them to the test. The next time you experience an intense emotion, try out one of your strategies from exercise 6.4. Use exercise 6.5 to keep track of how well each of the activities you identified works for you. In the first column, enter all of the self-soothing strategies you identified in exercise 6.4. Then, the next time you feel upset, try using one of these strategies. First, rate your level of distress on a scale from 0 (completely calm) to 10 (incredibly distressed) and put your rating in the "Distress Before" column. Then, after you use the skill, immediately rate your distress again on a scale from 0 to 10 in the "Distress After" column. This will help you figure out which of the strategies work best for you.

Exercise 6.5. Practicing Self-Soothing Skills

Self-Soothing Strategy	Distress Before (0–10)	Distress After (0–10)
Touch		
1.		
2.		
3.		
4.		
5.		
Taste		
1.		
2.		
3.		
4.		
5.		

Self-Soothing Strategy	Distress Before (0–10)	Distress After (0–10)
Smell		
1.		
2.		
3.		
4.		
5.		
Sight		
1.		
2.		
3.		
4.		
5.		

Self-Soothing Strategy	Distress Before (0–10)	Distress After (0–10)
Hearing		
1.		
2.		
3.		
4.		
5.		

Specific Skills for Managing Anger

All of the skills we described above can be helpful for managing anger. Just like the emotions of fear, sadness, guilt, and joy, anger is a basic human emotion that all people experience. And, just like these other emotions, anger serves an important purpose. Anger can give you the motivation you need to tackle problems head on; it gives you the strength to stand up for yourself and others. It can also signal when something isn't going well in your life and motivate you to change things. Therefore, mindfully observing your anger and its components and identifying the information it's providing can be useful skills.

As helpful as anger can be, however, it can also be difficult to manage. Many of the action urges associated with anger involve behaviors that are somewhat destructive. For this reason, when anger is intense, it can be difficult to avoid acting in ways that you'll later regret. Therefore, one of the best skills for managing intense anger is the dialectical behavior therapy skill of distraction that we reviewed above (Linehan 1993b, 2015). Using this skill will give your anger time to subside. It will also keep you from inadvertently re-triggering your anger by ruminating about what made you angry.

Beyond the skills we've already reviewed, however, there are two other simple strategies for managing intense anger that can be helpful for people with PTSD.

Leave the Situation

One of the best strategies for managing intense anger is also the simplest: leave the situation. Although simple, this can be an incredibly powerful tool, providing the time and space you need to figure out how best to respond, and giving your anger a chance to become less intense. Although it may sometimes feel like your anger will last forever, emotions are not long-lasting. They peak and subside, and, no matter how intense they feel in any given moment, they always pass. Therefore, simply buying some time will give your anger a chance to begin to subside. Leaving the situation will also provide some distance between you and the situation that elicited your anger so that it doesn't keep getting triggered.

Stop and Take a Step Back

Although leaving the situation when you're really angry can be a very useful skill, there will be times when it just isn't possible to leave the situation, or when leaving a situation has its own downsides. You may be in a moving car with someone, on a plane, in an important meeting at work, or with young children who need constant supervision. In situations like these, when you can't physically leave the situation, one of the most effective ways to avoid making things worse is to simply stop, take a moment, and take a step back from the situation (Linehan 2015). Pausing before you act and giving yourself a moment to figure out what to do next is a simple yet powerful strategy for managing intense anger effectively (Linehan 2015). Follow the steps below to practice this skill.

1. Stop what you're doing. Don't make a move. Don't open your mouth. Just stop in your tracks.

2. Take a moment to center yourself. Allow yourself a brief pause. Take a deep breath. Count to ten in your mind. Or try some of the skills for keeping your mind busy that we described earlier.

3. Take a step back from the situation and notice what you're experiencing. Apply the mindfulness skills of attending to and objectively labeling your experience to get a better understanding of what is happening.

4. Think through the consequences of reacting out of anger or acting on urges to do something destructive or, alternatively, choosing not to act on these urges but to respond more effectively instead.

5. Choose how to proceed. Think about what will be most effective in the long term. If your anger is getting in the way of thinking clearly, use the distraction skills from this chapter to distract yourself from your anger and give it time to pass. Continue to refrain from acting until you are able to leave the situation or your anger subsides.

The next time you're experiencing anger and at risk for doing something you'll regret, try this skill. You'll be amazed at just how powerful stopping in your tracks and taking a step back can be. Even if this buys you only a few minutes between having the action urge and acting on it, this can be enough time to connect with the downsides of acting on anger urges and make a different choice.

Skills for Managing Shame

As we mentioned previously, most emotions that people experience are helpful. Even if they feel overwhelming, emotions serve an important purpose and provide useful information. That's why so many of the most useful skills for regulating emotions focus on experiencing emotions and identifying the information they provide. There is one notable exception to this rule, however, and that is the emotion of shame. Although the vast majority of emotions that people experience are functional, shame is far less helpful. And this means that the best skills for managing shame are different from a lot of the skills we've reviewed in this chapter so far.

So, what exactly is shame? Well, shame is an emotion that stems from negative evaluations or judgments of you as a person. Unlike the emotion of guilt, which stems from negative evaluations of specific things you said or did, shame comes up when you judge yourself as a whole. And that's why shame isn't helpful. Not only does it go along with self-hatred and low self-worth, it can actually get in the way of changing problematic behaviors. Think about it—if you think that you're a decent person who sometimes does things that aren't okay, you may be motivated to work on changing behaviors that you don't like. If you think that you're just a terrible person all around, however, it's hard to imagine that things could ever change. When you feel shame, it's easy to believe that there isn't much point in working on changing your behavior. Shame keeps people stuck.

Unfortunately, shame is also incredibly common among people with PTSD. In fact, it's so common that shame is now included as one of the diagnostic criteria for this disorder. For this reason, it's important to know specific strategies for managing shame. And the most helpful one of all is the dialectical behavior therapy skill of *opposite action* (Linehan 1993b, 2015).

Opposite Action

In a nutshell, opposite action involves doing the opposite of the action urges that go along with an emotion. Doing this keeps the emotion from intensifying and helps it pass. This skill is best for managing emotions that are not helpful. And since shame is really never helpful, it's the strategy we recommend the most for this emotion. To practice this skill, you need to first identify the action urges that go along with the emotion. For shame, the action urges are to hide, avoid, shut down, and self-punish. Therefore, one way to act counter to these urges is simply not to avoid or hide. Approach other people. Look them in the eye. Tell a trusted friend or therapist about your traumatic experience. Continue to reach out to others and surround yourself with people you care about. Do your best to avoid isolating yourself. As difficult as it may be to resist the urges to avoid, doing so will definitely help you reduce feelings of shame.

Another opposite action for shame is to treat yourself with compassion and kindness. Shame makes people want to beat themselves up and punish themselves. The opposite of this is to treat yourself with respect and to practice self-compassion. Specific strategies for practicing self-compassion are listed below.

- *Do something nice for yourself.* Even if you don't *feel* loving toward yourself in the moment, you can *behave* lovingly by doing something kind for yourself. Give yourself a gift, treat yourself to your favorite meal or snack, watch your favorite television show or movie, or practice some of the self-soothing strategies we described earlier. Acting as if you love and respect yourself is one way to elicit those feelings and increase self-compassion.

- *Focus on your strengths and positive characteristics.* Focus your attention on the things you like about yourself, your positive behaviors, and all the things you do that have positive consequences for others. Think about the steps you've been taking to improve your life and gain more skills. Recognize your accomplishments and the parts of yourself that you appreciate. Focusing on your positive characteristics and strengths can be encouraging and can motivate you to make important changes. In contrast, beating yourself up is demoralizing and makes it less likely that you'll take steps to improve your life.

Moving Forward

Persistent negative emotions are one of the symptoms of PTSD, and they are incredibly common among people who struggle with this disorder. Along with the intense fear and anxiety that are at the core of this disorder, people with PTSD often struggle with a number of intense emotions that can be difficult to regulate, including anger and shame. This chapter described a number of different skills for regulating intense emotions, from mindfully observing and better understanding your emotions to focusing your attention on something else. We also described skills for managing the specific emotions of anger and shame, including taking a step back from the situation (literally or figuratively) when experiencing anger and acting opposite to the action urges of shame by treating yourself with kindness and compassion. Think of these skills as ammunition in your arsenal for managing intense emotions. The more skills at your disposal, the better able you'll be to manage any intense emotions that arise. The key to regulating emotions effectively is having a number of different strategies to choose from, depending on the situation and your goals in the moment. Keep practicing the skills in this chapter, and you'll experience their benefits firsthand.

CHAPTER 7

Preventing Reckless and Self-Destructive Behavior

With the publication of the fifth edition of the *Diagnostic and Statistical Manual of Mental Disorders* in 2013, a new symptom was added to the PTSD diagnosis—reckless and self-destructive behavior. A number of studies show that there is something about PTSD that increases the likelihood that a person will engage in a variety of impulsive, risky, or self-destructive behaviors. Self-injury, binge eating, substance abuse, and risky sexual behavior are all more common among people with PTSD (Brady, Back, and Coffey 2004; Brewerton 2007; Dixon-Gordon, Tull, and Gratz 2014; Weiss et al. 2012).

Now, you may wonder why someone would engage in behaviors that clearly have some serious downsides to them. There are actually a number of reasons why these behaviors may occur and why they can be so difficult to resist. Earlier, when we talked about avoidance behaviors, we mentioned that our behavior is largely influenced by its short-term consequences. That is, if something positive occurs or if something unpleasant is taken away when you engage in a certain behavior, you will be much more likely to repeat that behavior in the future, even if you know that it may cause some problems for you down the road. This is exactly what happens with reckless and self-destructive behavior. Some of these behaviors can be viewed as a form of *self-medication*, a way of getting relief from unpleasant PTSD symptoms. Excessive drinking or drug use may block out certain thoughts, memories, or feelings, or it may allow you to fall asleep quicker. Binge eating or risky sexual behavior may reduce emotional numbness by causing you to feel some positive emotions. Cutting or burning yourself may release tension or distract you from the emotional pain you are feeling.

Another reason why these behaviors may be more likely to occur among people with PTSD is that when you are putting all of your effort into managing intense and unpleasant thoughts and emotions, you have fewer resources available to control other behaviors. You can think of your ability to regulate your thoughts, emotions, and behaviors as a muscle—it is a limited resource. Because intense emotions, thoughts, and memories frequently occur in PTSD, that muscle is being constantly taxed. It takes a lot of energy to manage those symptoms. As a result, you may have more difficulty resisting urges to engage in unhealthy and self-destructive behaviors.

Some of these self-destructive behaviors may also be driven by negative thoughts or beliefs that commonly occur in PTSD. As we discussed in chapter 4, people with PTSD may develop thoughts of hopelessness or helplessness: *Things will never get better* or *There's no point in trying.* Buying into these thoughts is dangerous, as they can cause you to not be concerned about the long-term consequences of your actions. If nothing will ever get better, what does it matter if a behavior leads to some negative outcome, such as continued distress or a damaged relationship? When emotional pain is great, immediate relief becomes the only priority.

Regardless of the cause, these behaviors can have a major negative impact on a number of different areas of your life. They can damage or end relationships. They can interfere with your ability to perform well at work or at school. They can also severely affect your mental and physical health. Given this, it is important to learn skills that can prevent these behaviors from occurring.

Increasing Your Motivation to Change a Self-Destructive Behavior

Self-destructive behaviors initially do something for you. They may help you get certain needs met, or they may give you much-needed relief from PTSD symptoms, even if that relief is temporary. Think about it—if these behaviors didn't help you in some way in the moment, you probably would choose not to engage in them. However, given that these behaviors can bring about some temporary relief, it may be hard to gather the motivation to change them. Fortunately, there are some ways to increase your motivation to change these unhealthy behaviors.

One thing that can drive self-destructive behaviors is focusing only on their short-term effects. When something positive happens after you do something, your mind connects that action with the outcome, making you more likely to repeat that behavior in the future. The long-term consequences, on the other hand, don't seem as connected to the behavior. They are too far removed from the action to have any immediate influence on your behavior when an urge is present. Therefore, one way to improve your ability to resist an urge for some self-destructive behavior is to remind yourself of its long-term negative consequences.

In exercise 7.1, we want you to close your eyes and think about the last time you engaged in a self-destructive behavior. How did you feel immediately after engaging in the behavior? What were the short-term positive and negative consequences of the behavior? For example, let's say that you cut yourself. You might write down that in the short term, you experienced some positive effects: reduced anxiety, distraction from unpleasant thoughts and memories, or the ability to feel something. You might have also noticed negative short-term consequences, such as having to hide the fact that you cut yourself or having to take care of your injury. Now think about the long-term consequences. Did your anxiety later get worse? Did you feel shame or guilt about not being able to resist the urge to cut yourself? You may have also noticed that your unpleasant thoughts came back or beliefs about being helpless got stronger. It is also possible that your self-destructive behavior interfered with relationships or with your ability to get things done at work and school. There can also be *positive* long-term consequences of a self-destructive behavior, and if they are there, it is important to recognize them. For example, some people say that some self-destructive behaviors, such as self-injury, may prevent even more severe behaviors, like suicide. If this is the case for you, make sure you write it down.

Exercise 7.1. Identifying Pros and Cons of a Self-Destructive Behavior

Behavior: _____	Positive	Negative
Short term		
Long term		

Once you are done with exercise 7.1, look it over. Do you notice that the short-term positive and long-term negative boxes are basically mirror images of each other? As much as self-destructive behaviors may help you initially escape distress, it is only a temporary fix, and the distress eventually comes back—sometimes even stronger. This then makes it more likely that a self-destructive behavior is going to occur again. Next time you feel a self-destructive urge, reread your answers here and remind yourself of the negative consequences of that behavior. Bringing those consequences to the forefront can help increase your motivation to resist the urge.

Another helpful exercise for increasing your motivation to stop a self-destructive behavior comes from a cognitive-behavioral treatment for impulse-control problems (Grant, Donahue, and Odlaug 2011). It can be helpful to think of what your life would be like without the self-destructive behavior. Look over your responses in the previous exercise. How have self-destructive behaviors affected your life? Have they affected your psychological or physical health? Have they caused problems in your relationships or your job? Have they made your PTSD symptoms worse? Imagine that there was a way you could immediately stop engaging in self-destructive behaviors. Imagine that all self-destructive behaviors and the urges to engage in these behaviors were erased from your life. What would your life look like? Write down your responses in exercise 7.2.

Exercise 7.2. Imagining Your Life Without Self-Destructive Behaviors

Work or school: _____

_____

Friendships: _____

_____

Romantic relationships: _____

_____

Family relationships: _____

_____

Finances: _____

_____

Physical health: _____

_____

Mental health: _____

_____

Leisure: _____

_____

Next time you feel a desire to engage in a self-destructive behavior, reread your responses in this exercise. You can even put it someplace where it is easily visible or accessible to you. Resisting the desire to engage in a self-destructive behavior can be a difficult thing to do, but this exercise can remind you why it is incredibly important that you do. Over time, as your self-destructive behaviors decrease, you may notice that your life is beginning to look a lot like what you wrote down.

Monitoring Your Urges to Engage in a Self-Destructive Behavior

Urges—desires or cravings—often precede a reckless or self-destructive behavior. They can be experienced in a number of different ways. Some urges feel like anxiety. You may notice muscle tension, nervous energy, racing thoughts, or a pounding heart. Other people can experience an urge as a feeling of hollowness or emptiness. Urges can also vary in strength. Some urges may come out of the blue and be overwhelming. These urges can hit you with so much force that you are caught off guard and feel out of control. Other urges may feel mild at first and slowly build over time.

In chapter 2, we discussed how you have to be aware of your triggers in order to deal with them. The same rule applies here: to best cope with your urges, you need to first know what they are. You need to know how you generally experience urges and when you may be more at risk for one. You can do this simply by tracking your urges to engage in self-destructive behaviors. Over time, if you can increase your awareness and keep track of them, they will begin to feel a little less unpredictable or uncontrollable. You will have a better idea of what brings about your urges, as well as how you experience them. In addition, if you know what types of things bring about your urges and when you may be more vulnerable to having them, you can then take steps ahead of time to prepare yourself to cope with them. Exercise 7.3 is a monitoring form that will help you track your urges (from *Freedom from Self-Harm* by Gratz and Chapman, 2009).

At the top of the form, write down what behavior you are targeting and describe the urges you experience for this behavior. For example, you may write: "Jittery, agitated, hot, heart racing." This will help you identify these urges in the future. Next, track these urges. Using a scale of 0–10—with 0 being no urges at all and 10 being the strongest you've ever had—rate how strong your urges are at different times of the day and evening, over the course of a week. (Feel free to modify the chart to fit your sleep schedule.) Finally, in the comments section of the exercise, write down what you were doing when you had the strongest urges. Also note if you were experiencing any particular emotions or thoughts at those times, such as intrusive memories or negative beliefs about yourself. Now step back and look at the urges as you tracked them over the course of a week. Can you see any patterns? Do you have the strongest urges at certain times of day or when you are experiencing certain emotions? If you do see a pattern, schedule time to use the skills we describe in this chapter (or elsewhere in this book) during those peak times when you expect to have the strongest urges.

Exercise 7.3. Keeping Track of Your Urges to Engage in a Self-Destructive Behavior

Self-destructive behavior:
What are your urges like for this behavior?

Track your urges:							
Day	8–10 a.m.	10 a.m.– noon	Noon– 2 p.m.	2–4 p.m.	4–6 p.m.	6–8 p.m.	8–10 p.m.
Monday							
Tuesday							
Wednesday							
Thursday							
Friday							
Saturday							
Sunday							
Comments							

Complete this exercise for each self-destructive behavior you struggle with. Different behaviors may be preceded by different types of urges, and different types of situations can bring on different types of urges and behaviors.

Substituting Healthy Behaviors for Unhealthy Behaviors

Self-destructive behaviors can do something important for you in the moment. They may provide you with emotional relief or a temporary break from unpleasant thoughts. Because of this, it is unrealistic to think that you can just stop engaging in them. Even though they may cause problems for you in the long run, self-destructive behaviors may help you address some important and valid needs. If you take away one method for meeting those needs without replacing it, you are likely going to feel more distress, which will only motivate a return to the very self-destructive behavior you wanted to stop (or even a worse one). Therefore, one way to prevent self-destructive behaviors is to identify healthy behaviors that can help you meet your needs. Revisit exercise 7.1, and look at the positive short-term consequences of your self-destructive behavior. That should give you some idea of the function your self-destructive behavior serves. What does it do for you in the moment? Does it help you manage unpleasant emotions? Does it help you fall asleep? Does it stop unpleasant thoughts or memories from flooding your mind? Does it bring about positive emotions?

Exercise 7.4 is designed to help you identify healthy replacements for these behaviors. In the first column, write down what your self-destructive behavior does for you in the short term. Then try to think about other activities that would have the same effect. Some of the skills discussed in previous chapters might be good candidates. For example, if your self-destructive behavior gives you some relief from unpleasant thoughts, you may write in "mindfulness of thoughts" (discussed in chapter 4) as a healthy alternative, as mindfulness can help reduce the power of unpleasant thoughts but not bring with it the long-term negative consequences of a self-destructive behavior. If you need help managing intense emotions, you might choose an emotion regulation skill from chapter 6. If you need to feel comforted, you could put in healthy activities that are soothing and comforting (such as taking a warm bubble bath). If you need to release tension, write in exercise, lifting weights, or another healthy activity that releases tension.

Exercise 7.4. Behavioral Substitutes for Self-Destructive Behaviors

What do your self-destructive behaviors do for you in the short term (what functions do they serve)?	What are some healthy behaviors that will help you meet these needs?
1.	1. 2. 3. 4.
2.	1. 2. 3. 4.
3.	1. 2. 3. 4.
4.	1. 2. 3. 4.
5.	1. 2. 3. 4.

For each function you identify in the first column, write down as many healthy behaviors as you possibly can. The more behaviors you identify, the easier it will be to resist an urge. It is also important to remember that the healthy alternatives you wrote down may not work as quickly or as completely as the self-destructive behavior. As we mentioned previously, self-destructive behaviors often bring relief very quickly—this is why they are so powerful and difficult to change. Healthy behaviors may not give you immediate relief, but they will give you some space from your suffering, and they will do so in a way that is not going to bring about additional problems for you down the road.

Distraction and Delay

By their very nature, urges to engage in self-destructive behaviors tend to be short-lived. Once an urge peaks in strength, it quickly begins to diminish. Nevertheless, intense urges can be hard to resist. They can grab your attention and feel as though they are going to last forever, and they may be extremely uncomfortable and unpleasant. When your urges peak, and if you have no tools ready to resist them, you will be more likely to give in and engage in a self-destructive behavior. However, if you can find some way to ride out that urge or distract yourself long enough from the urge, it should go away (or at least weaken) rather quickly, making it easier to withstand. This next set of skills is focused on helping you find ways to distract yourself from an urge or ride it out.

We discussed distraction in chapter 2, as a way of dealing with PTSD triggers, and in chapter 6, in talking about how to manage intense emotions. Distraction is also a useful skill when it comes to urges. Like triggers and intense emotions, urges grab your attention, and the more you focus on an urge, the more intense it may feel. This makes it difficult to resist. However, if you can find something else to do while you are experiencing an urge, it is less likely that you will be pulled in. This will allow the urge to peak and then decline on its own.

When coming up with distraction strategies, you want to find activities that are healthy, engaging, and meaningful to you. A boring activity isn't going to pull your attention away from an urge, and you want to make sure you are not distracting yourself with another self-destructive behavior. Doing something enjoyable that requires your full focus is going to be most successful. Completing a word puzzle, talking to a friend, reading a book, doing arts and crafts, or playing with a pet are all activities that require some level of concentration and can capture your attention. You can also distract yourself by focusing on your five senses, as was discussed in chapter 6. You can suck on a strong peppermint candy or touch something with a unique texture. You can smell a strongly scented candle or listen to loud music. All of these activities will compete with the urge by grabbing your attention.

Another useful skill for riding out an urge is delaying responding to the urge. Because urges are short-lived, if you can delay acting on the urge just a little bit, chances are the urge will weaken enough that it will be easier not to give in to it. For example, you could set a timer and challenge yourself to not act on the urge for ten minutes. Once those ten minutes are up, you can revisit your desire to engage in a self-destructive behavior. For some self-destructive behaviors, you can also simply make them more difficult to do. For example, if you struggle with drinking, make sure no alcohol is readily accessible to you. If there is alcohol in your house, ask other people in your home to lock it up or put it in a place where you cannot easily get it. If you engage in impulsive spending, you can literally freeze your credit cards in a block of ice. Or, if you struggle with self-injury, you can make sure that the implements you use (such as scissors, a knife, or a lighter) are locked up or put someplace where it takes some time to get to them (like in the trunk of your car in the garage). The basic idea is that you want to make it more difficult to engage in a self-destructive behavior when you experience an urge. The more time you put between an urge and the opportunity to engage in a self-destructive behavior, the more time the urge has to decrease in intensity, making it easier for you to resist that urge.

In exercise 7.5 below, brainstorm and write down some healthy distraction and delay activities that you think would work best for you. When you have a list, ask yourself when the best time would be to engage in these activities. Some activities might work better than others in certain situations. For example, if you are in the middle of a meeting at work and you notice an urge to self-injure, arts and crafts is likely not going to be the most effective distraction activity. If you are alone, however, arts and crafts may work very well. It is also possible that some activities will work better only for certain types of urges. For instance, you may find that delay activities work best for urges to drink but not so well for urges to binge eat. In the end, you want to identify distraction and delay activities that could be used in a number of different situations. The more situations you cover, the better prepared you will be to cope with urges.

Exercise 7.5. Distraction and Delay

Distraction Activities	Best Times or Situations to Use Strategy
1.	1. 2. 3.
2.	1. 2. 3.
3.	1. 2. 3.
4.	1. 2. 3.
5.	1. 2. 3.

Delay Activities	Best Times or Situations to Use Strategy
1.	1. 2. 3.
2.	1. 2. 3.
3.	1. 2. 3.
4.	1. 2. 3.
5.	1. 2. 3.

Practice Mindfulness to Manage Urges

Another way to cope with urges is to be mindful of your urges. Even though urges can be unpleasant to experience, observing them in a nonjudgmental way can reduce some of their power and make them pass much more quickly. In fact, some treatments for people who struggle with alcohol and drug use place a major emphasis on using mindfulness to cope with urges (mindfulness-based relapse prevention; Witkiewitz, Marlatt, and Walker 2005). One skill from this treatment is called *urge surfing*, which is described in exercise 7.6 (from *Freedom from Self-Harm* by Gratz and Chapman, 2009).

Find a quiet place where you are relatively free from distractions. Sit in a comfortable position. Write down how strong your urge is on a scale from 0 (no urge at all) to 10 (the strongest urge you have ever had). Then, write down how much you feel you can handle your urge on a scale from 0 (can't take it for one more second) to 10 (could handle it for a long time if you had to).

Now imagine that you are standing on a surfboard in the ocean in a warm, tropical place. You can see the sandy white shore in front of you, there's a slight breeze, and you can smell the salt of the ocean. There are a few fluffy white clouds overhead, and the sun feels warm on your back. Really transport your mind to this scene. Now, imagine that your urge to engage in a self-destructive behavior is the wave that you're riding. Notice in detail what the urge feels like in your body. Zero in on the sensations you feel (for example, a racing heart or muscle tension). Now imagine that you're surfing the wave, and the wave is your urge. As your urge rises and becomes stronger, the wave gets higher, but you keep surfing on top of it. Imagine that you're an excellent surfer who can handle any wave that comes your way. As the urge gets stronger and stronger, the wave gets higher and higher, until it crests. Imagine that you're riding the wave to the shore. As you watch and surf the wave, notice what happens to it. Does it get higher and stronger, or does it start getting lower and weaker? When it gets weaker, imagine that you're gliding with your surfboard to shore. When it starts to build again, imagine that you're back out there on the wave, just riding it. Keep doing this for about ten minutes or so, or until you feel as if you have a handle on the urge and will not act on it.

At the end, write down how strong your urge is on a scale from 0 to 10 and how much you feel you can handle your urge on a scale from 0 to 10.

Exercise 7.6. Mindfully Observing Your Urges: Urge Surfing

Urge	Strength of Urge Before (0–10)	How Much You Can Handle the Urge (0–10)	Strength of Urge After (0–10)

Also, keep in mind that if using the imagery of an ocean wave doesn't work for you, you can also do this exercise by simply noticing how the physical feelings and sensations of the urge come and go.

The great thing about urge surfing (and mindfulness in general) is that you can practice this skill pretty much anywhere and anytime. This makes it a versatile skill when it comes to dealing with urges for self-destructive behaviors. Urge surfing is also a great skill in that it can actually

127

help increase your tolerance of urges. By sitting with your urges and not reacting to them, you notice that they are relatively short-lived and will pass on their own. In this way, urge surfing can also be considered a form of exposure, which was discussed in chapter 5. The more you come into contact with urges and ride them out, the less frightening and overwhelming they will seem. By not giving in to the urges, you are teaching your brain that urges aren't going to work anymore. This means that over time, the urges should actually reduce in intensity and eventually may not even occur.

Some Additional Points

As you move forward in coping with urges to engage in self-destructive behaviors, there are a few other things that you want to keep in mind.

- It is not easy to resist an urge to engage in a self-destructive behavior. In fact, it may be incredibly unpleasant to do so. Urges can be associated with strong bodily arousal (for example, muscle tension or increased heart rate), racing thoughts, and anxiety. In addition, if you resist engaging in a self-destructive behavior, you aren't going to get the short-term positive consequence of engaging in that behavior. Therefore, you want to find ways to reward yourself for resisting an urge to engage in a self-destructive behavior. The reward doesn't have to be large—just something that recognizes that you did something that was challenging and difficult. You may put aside some time to engage in an activity that you really enjoy. Or you may decide to splurge a little and buy yourself your favorite coffee or download a song you like. You might simply put a star on a calendar everytime you resist an urge, and when you've earned enough stars, give yourself a bigger reward. Maybe seeing how many times you were able to resist urges over a period of time will be rewarding in and of itself.

- You want to be on the lookout for the *rule violation effect*, which occurs when we set hard-and-fast rules for ourselves that can be difficult to follow. For example, you may tell yourself that you can never engage in a self-destructive behavior again. But as we've discussed, it can be difficult to resist urges, and you might violate or break your rules, especially early on, when you are still learning the skills covered in this book. Given that these are all-or-none rules, once the rule is broken, the motivation to resist the urge is seriously weakened. For example, imagine someone is trying to quit smoking, and he tells himself that he can never have a cigarette again. On one stressful day, however, he gives in to an urge and takes a few drags off a cigarette. The rule has now been broken, so he thinks to himself, *Well, I've smoked, so I might as well just go ahead and finish the entire cigarette.* Giving in to these types of thoughts is dangerous, because the more you engage in a self-destructive behavior, the harder it is going to be to resist in the future. Violating these kinds of rules can also bring up shame, guilt, and other unpleasant emotions that may increase the urges. Instead of setting hard-and-fast rules, commit to the moment-by-moment process of abstaining from the self-destructive behavior. If you happen to slip, recognize it as simply that—a slip. Use this lapse as an opportunity to better prepare yourself for dealing with future urges. Identify what it was that caused you to slip and try to think about what you could do next time you are in a similar situation to prevent a slip from occurring. And practice self-compassion—resisting urges is not an easy thing to do.

- Finally, a lot of our behavior is influenced by our environment, both external and internal. Some self-destructive behaviors may be more likely in certain situations, at certain times, or when you are having specific emotions or thoughts. Try to identify *high-risk situations*—where you may be more at risk for urges. Some situations can be avoided. If you have a problem with drinking, stay out of bars. Many situations, however, aren't easy to avoid. Using the skills in this chapter and book, plan ahead for how you can cope with your high-risk situations.

Moving Forward

Reckless and self-destructive behaviors can have a major negative impact on your life and your PTSD symptoms. In fact, some of these behaviors may even increase the likelihood that you'll experience another traumatic event. For example, if you decide to drive after a night of heavy drinking, you'll be at much greater risk for an accident or severely injuring someone. For this reason, if you struggle with reckless and self-destructive behaviors, it is important to learn ways of preventing them. In this chapter, you learned ways to increase your motivation to stop self-destructive behaviors. You've also learned several ways of coping with urges to engage in them. In addition to the skills in this chapter, it may be helpful to think about how skills discussed in other chapters may help reduce self-destructive behaviors. For example, emotion regulation skills (chapter 6) may help you better manage the intense emotions that tend to precede self-destructive behaviors. Behavioral activation (chapter 10) may increase your sense of hope and may make you feel more in control of and connected with your life, reducing the desire to engage in reckless or risky behaviors. Using skills for coping with negative beliefs (chapter 4) may address unpleasant thoughts. As we've said before, self-destructive behaviors can be difficult to deal with; the more skills you have available, the better off you will be in preventing them from occurring.

CHAPTER 8

Improving Your Sleep: The Fundamentals

PTSD and sleep difficulties go hand in hand. Studies show that sleep difficulties are among the most common problems experienced by people with PTSD (Babson and Feldner 2010). Indeed, approximately 70 percent have periodic sleep problems (Ohayon and Shapiro 2000). As we've mentioned, some of the core symptoms of PTSD include hyperarousal, irritability, nightmares, and flashbacks; these symptoms directly interfere with sleep. In addition, sleep difficulties can make your symptoms worse. For example, people who experience insomnia often feel keyed up, on edge, and "wired but tired" during the day; they feel hyperaroused. If you have PTSD, you probably already feel hyperaroused, so the extra agitation stemming from insomnia only makes matters worse. Fortunately, some key skills and strategies can help you to improve your sleep and reduce PTSD-related sleep problems. In this chapter, we will focus on ways to establish a strong foundation of sleep habits. Our suggestions come largely from the latest work on cognitive-behavioral therapy for insomnia, an extremely effective treatment for people who have sleep problems (Morin et al. 2006). This chapter will help you to level the playing field and ensure that you are well equipped to use our advice in the next chapter, which focuses on nightmares and other sleep problems associated with PTSD.

Understanding How Sleep Works

To improve your sleep, you first need to know a little about how sleep works. The first and most important thing to know is that human beings need sleep. Sleep is as important as food, water, and other necessities. Sleep helps repair and grow new cells in your body, helps organize your memories and the things that you've learned, and helps you function throughout the day. When you've slept well, you feel refreshed, alert, able to pay attention and manage your emotions, capable of handling stress, and able to think clearly. Prolonged sleep deprivation, on the other hand, can lead to depression, difficulty staying awake during the day, agitation, physical health problems, hallucinations, and even death (Kripke, Marler, and Calle 2004). People who do shift work, and thus have sleep cycles that are chronically disrupted, are at elevated risk for cancer and cardiovascular and metabolic diseases (Kripke, Marler, and Calle 2004). Sleep is a critical bodily function. We need it to function and survive.

Perhaps because sleep is so important to our well-being and survival, our bodies and brains have systems to manage sleep. One of these systems is the twenty-four-hour biological clock often called the *circadian clock* or *circadian rhythm*. The circadian clock influences when we fall asleep, when we enter particular stages of sleep, and when we become alert and awake. Human beings are *diurnal*, meaning that their circadian clocks are set for daytime wakefulness and nighttime sleep. Some other animals, such as guinea pigs, are nocturnal; they sleep during the day and are awake at night. No matter how much of a night owl (or guinea pig) you are, your circadian clock will still tell your body and brain that nighttime is the time to sleep and daytime is the time to be awake. This is why many researchers believe that shift work involving night or graveyard shifts is harmful and impossible to sustain without causing health problems in the long term.

Sleep drive is another system that regulates sleep. A lot like the biological drives related to hunger, thirst, or sex, sleep drive is basically the need for sleep. The longer you go without liquid, the thirstier you become. The longer you go without sleep, the more your sleep drive builds—the more you need sleep. When your sleep drive is high, you will feel an overpowering urge to fall asleep. You will probably experience lapses in your concentration, like when you're watching a television show and realize you just missed the last couple of minutes. You will also probably feel the urge to close your eyes or to nod off. In other words, you will become sleepy. Sleepiness is related to the buildup of sleep drive.

As long as everything is going as it should, your sleep drive will help ensure that you go to bed at a reasonable time, one that fits your circadian clock, and that you get plenty of restorative sleep. Normally, sleep drive is at its lowest as you awaken in the morning, and it starts to build up during the day, peaking right around the time that you go to bed. If you have built up enough sleep drive during the day, you will start to feel sleepy as bedtime approaches, and you will nod off pretty quickly—on average, within about thirty minutes of going to bed. Your sleep quality will be good, and you'll spend time in restorative sleep.

Increasing Your Chances of a Quality Sleep

If you're struggling with PTSD, an important first step in addressing sleep problems is to make sure you have a strong foundation of healthy sleep habits that will allow your natural sleep systems to do what they do best. If you're generally trying to sleep at a time that fits your unique circadian clock and building up enough sleep drive, you will be one step closer to having consistent, higher quality sleep. The good news is that you can start taking this step and laying down a strong foundation right away. In this section, we will talk about ways to work with your circadian clock and ways to maximize sleep drive.

Working with Your Circadian Clock

One common contributor to poor sleep is a sleep schedule that is out of sync with your circadian rhythm. While all humans are diurnal, each person is wired slightly differently; some stay up late, others fall asleep earlier. If you are a night owl, and you're regularly trying to go to bed early or to get up at first light, you might also find that you're struggling to fall sleep at night and having difficulty waking up in the morning. In addition, your sleep quality will suffer. You probably won't spend enough time in restorative sleep, and you might end up feeling stressed and not very alert during the day. Therefore, one of the first steps in improving your sleep is to determine what kind of sleeper you are. Once you've done that, you can build a sleep schedule that best fits your clock.

The best way to determine your circadian clock is to start keeping track of your sleep using a sleep diary. Exercise 8.1 is an example of a sleep diary that you can use to keep track of your sleep, determine what kind of sleeper you are, and figure out how much sleep you seem to need. Consider filling this out for at least two or three weeks, so that you can get a good sample of your sleep patterns.

Exercise 8.1. Sleep Diary

Day	Mon.	Tues.	Wed.	Thurs.	Fri.	Sat.	Sun.
What time did you go to bed?	11 p.m.						
What time did you fall asleep?	12 a.m.						
Number of times you woke up	3 times						
How long, in total, were you awake?	1 hour						
What time did you finally wake up for the day?	6 a.m.						
What time did you get out of bed for the day?	7:15 a.m.						
What was the quality of your sleep?	Poor						
How sleepy did you feel during the day?	3/5						
What was your mood like during the day?	1/5						
How alert did you feel during the day?	2/5						

1. *Figure out how much, on average, you're sleeping each night.* It's a myth that everyone needs eight hours of sleep. Different people need different amounts of sleep; researchers have discovered that, on average, people probably need somewhere between seven and nine hours per night. Once you figure out how much you're sleeping on average, you'll have a good idea of approximately how much sleep you need.

2. *Check your ratings of the quality of your sleep.* Is there any relationship between your sleep quality and when you went to bed and woke up? You might, for example, notice that when you sleep from eleven at night until seven in the morning, you feel your sleep quality was good, but when you sleep from one in the morning until nine, the quality of your sleep is lower. Others may find they sleep best from midnight to eight, from nine to five, or some other range of times.

3. *Look at your ratings of your mood, how sleepy you were, and how alert you felt throughout the day.* For your mood, use a rating from 1 (low mood, miserable) to 5 (excited, happy, joyous); for sleepiness, from 1 (no energy, very sleepy) to 5 (lots of energy, not sleepy at all); and finally, for alertness, from 1 (not alert at all) to 5 (extremely alert). If you were quite sleepy, did not feel alert, and your mood was low during the day, it's possible that you were not sleeping at the right time. Keep in mind, however, that if you have insomnia, you might not feel sleepy. Instead, you might feel tired and wired. Also, look at how much you're sleeping. If you feel rested and alert, and you function well on seven hours of sleep, perhaps that's the amount you need. Or you may feel that way only after eight or nine hours of sleep.

4. *Once you have a good idea of how much sleep you need and approximately when it's best for you to sleep, the next challenge is to create a consistent sleep schedule.* Generally, it's best to awaken at approximately the same time every morning and to go to bed when you feel sleepy. Set a wake-up time that best matches your circadian rhythm given work and other external schedules. Use an alarm clock, and set it for the same time each day. When the alarm goes off, do your best to get out of bed as soon as you can. Try to have a general idea of your bedtime (e.g., between ten thirty and eleven if you plan to wake up at seven), but it's more important to have a consistent wake-up time than it is to have the exact same bedtime every night.

Optimizing Your Sleep Drive

In order to experience quality, restorative sleep, you need to build up sleep drive—the need for sleep—during the day. Many things can influence your sleep drive, including the number of hours you've been awake, whether you took a nap during the day, the time of day, exposure to light, consumption of caffeine or other substances, and your level of activity throughout the day. Here are a few questions that will help you figure out what you need to work on in order to improve your sleep drive.

When do you generally wake up in the morning on weekdays?

- ☐ 5–6 a.m.
- ☐ 6–7 a.m.
- ☐ 7–8 a.m.
- ☐ 8–9 a.m.
- ☐ 9–10 a.m.
- ☐ 10 a.m. or later
- ☐ Other
- ☐ My wake-up time changes by an hour or more each day.

When do you generally wake up in the morning on weekends?

- ☐ 5–6 a.m.
- ☐ 6–7 a.m.
- ☐ 7–8 a.m.
- ☐ 8–9 a.m.
- ☐ 9–10 a.m.
- ☐ 10 a.m. or later
- ☐ Other
- ☐ My wake-up time changes by an hour or more each day.

These are two of the most important questions to consider when evaluating your sleep drive. If you answered that your wake-up time changes by an hour or more each day, you are probably not optimizing your sleep drive. Let's say you wake up at seven and go to bed at eleven on Wednesday. You've discovered that you need about seven and a half to eight hours of sleep, which means you normally would have about sixteen hours to build up adequate sleep drive. On Thursday, however, you don't have to go to work until later, so you sleep in until eight thirty. By the time you would normally go to bed, you will probably not have built up enough sleep drive to fall asleep quickly and dive into restorative sleep. As a result, you might have difficulty falling asleep, and you might be more prone to wake up in the middle of the night. The bottom line here is that your wake-up time sets your bedtime. A consistent wake-up time allows you to build up sleep drive during the day.

Sleep experts recommend that you should wake up at about the same time every day, even on weekends. If you change your wake-up time dramatically on the weekend, you are creating a situation similar to jet lag. It's like you've entered a different time zone, and your sleep cycle will be out of sync with your normal circadian rhythm. As a result, you will not build up enough sleep drive to go to sleep at a normal time, and when Sunday comes around, you might have difficulty getting to sleep at a time that will allow you to feel restored, refreshed, and able to face work on Monday morning.

What do you do if you feel like you didn't get a good night's sleep?

- ☐ I take a nap during the day.

- ☐ I go to bed earlier the next day.

- ☐ I sleep in later the next morning.

- ☐ I go to bed and get up at my regular time.

- ☐ I try to do less activity during the day.

- ☐ I try to get less exercise during the day.

- ☐ I rest a lot to recover from the bad night.

After what we said in the previous section, you can probably guess what we'll say here. It is tempting to make up for a poor night's sleep by napping, changing your bedtime, taking it easy with activities, or sleeping in. Although these efforts may seem like a good idea at the time, they actually can undermine your sleep. We will discuss napping and activity level below and focus here on the importance of consistency in your sleep schedule. If you didn't sleep well, the best thing to do the next day is to simply go to bed close to your regular bedtime and to wake up at your regular time. Even though you might have a sleep deficit from not getting enough sleep the night before, your brain will help you make up for it without the need for you to sleep in or go to bed early. Contrary to what many people think, you don't need to sleep longer to make up for your lack of sleep. You will naturally make up for lost sleep by spending more time in restorative sleep the next night. If you normally sleep for seven to eight hours, those seven to eight hours will be more full of restorative sleep than usual, helping you make up for the previous night.

How many caffeinated beverages (coffee, tea, or soda) do you consume each day?

- [ ] 0 cups or glasses

- [ ] Less than 1 cup or glass

- [ ] 1–2 cups or glasses

- [ ] 3–4 cups or glasses

- [ ] More than 4 cups or glasses

Coffee and other caffeinated beverages are not necessarily bad for your sleep, but sleep researchers believe that caffeine can reduce the buildup of sleep drive. As you engage in activities throughout the day, a certain chemical called *adenosine* builds up in your cells and certain areas of your brain. When you sleep, adenosine gradually decreases, until you wake up, and then it starts to build again. Does this sound similar to what we said about sleep drive? Sleep scientists believe that adenosine plays an important role in sleep and wakefulness, and that things that reduce adenosine might reduce sleep drive. It turns out that caffeine can reduce the buildup of adenosine. It is not clear as to how much caffeine you can consume before it begins to have a detrimental effect on your sleep drive, but if you have several cups of coffee (or other caffeinated beverages) per day, we hope this is food (or drink) for thought. You might consider experimenting with fewer caffeinated drinks and see if it helps you feel sleepier around bedtime and get more restorative sleep during the night.

How regularly do you nap?

- ☐ Never

- ☐ Rarely—1–2 times per month or fewer

- ☐ 1–2 times per week

- ☐ 3–4 times per week

- ☐ 5–7 times per week

How long are your naps?

- ☐ I don't nap.

- ☐ 5–15 minutes

- ☐ 16–20 minutes

- ☐ 21–30 minutes

- ☐ 31–60 minutes

- ☐ More than 60 minutes

Napping is not generally considered bad for your sleep unless you have sleep problems. If you have insomnia, however, napping is a lot like smoking when you have asthma. When you nap during the day, you tend to spend that time in relatively light stages of sleep (often referred to as stage 1 or 2). As a result, napping doesn't have the same restorative effects as sleeping at night, when you're likely to spend a lot more time in what's called *slow-wave sleep* (stages 3 and 4), the most restorative type of sleep. What napping does, however, is rob your sleep drive and that night's sleep will suffer.

- ☐ You might not feel sleepy at your regular bedtime.

- ☐ You might spend less time in restorative slow-wave sleep.

- ☐ You might be more likely to wake up in the night.

As a result, for people with sleep problems (such as those with PTSD), napping is a bad deal. Although you might experience some short-term benefits from napping, the long-term costs are generally not worth it. If someone said, "I'll either give you $10 now or $100 at ten o'clock tonight," what would you do? If you were sure the person would return at ten to give you $100, you'd be much better off saying no to the $10 now. Napping is like taking the $10 now.

How close to bedtime do you use electronic devices emitting blue-spectrum light (tablets, smartphones, laptops, desktop computers, television, and energy-efficient lightbulbs)?

- [ ] More than 3 hours before bedtime

- [ ] 1–2 hours before bedtime

- [ ] 31–60 minutes before bedtime

- [ ] 16–30 minutes before bedtime

- [ ] 5–15 minutes before bedtime

- [ ] In bed

Studies have shown that exposure to blue-spectrum light can suppress the secretion of a hormone called *melatonin* (Figueiro et al. 2011). Melatonin plays an important role in regulating the sleep and wakefulness cycle, so reducing your melatonin levels may jeopardize your sleep quality. Ideally, you should limit your exposure to blue-spectrum light in the hours before bedtime. You might, for example, set a cutoff time after which you don't allow yourself to check email, watch television, surf the Internet, and so on. Try to avoid keeping your smartphone or other mobile device in your bedroom. If you use your phone as an alarm clock, put it in airplane mode (to discourage you from checking mail or going online in bed), place your phone out of reach, or turn off your Wi-Fi before you go to bed—or you could consider purchasing an old-fashioned alarm clock or clock radio. Avoid watching television close to bedtime, unless doing so is part of your bedtime routine. If television helps you unwind and doesn't seem to be delaying sleepiness, you might not need to be concerned with it. If you must use computers or other devices in the hour or two before bedtime, consider using a setting or an app that changes the type of light these devices emit.

How active are you throughout the day?

☐   Not very active—mostly sedentary, spending most of the day sitting

☐   Somewhat active—working or volunteering regularly, seeing people occasionally, walking from the car or bus to work

☐   Moderately active—walking regularly, seeing people, working or volunteering, engaging in recreational activities, exercising a few times per week

☐   Quite active—working or volunteering daily, seeing or interacting with others regularly, exercising for twenty minutes or more per day

☐   Extremely active—working or volunteering daily, lots of interaction with other people, engaging in recreational or hobby activities, exercising for thirty minutes to an hour or more per day

Activity during the day can promote restorative sleep at night. You can think of slow-wave sleep as your brain's and body's way of recovering from the activities of your day. If you've had an active, stimulating day, you'll probably need more slow-wave sleep. You will probably build up more sleep drive than you would if you had a less active day. Try to make sure you have an active life and stimulating things to do during the day, and minimize time spent at sedentary activities. Consider taking public transportation or cycling to and from work or school, and schedule regular exercise for yourself, even if it's just for a short period. It's totally fine to have downtime, to relax, watch television, surf the Internet, and so on, but try to balance these activities with walking, exercise, working, or socializing. Research has long shown that exercise improves your sleep, and it is now beginning to show that exercise can be particularly beneficial for people with PTSD (Asmundson et al. 2013; Manger and Motta 2005).

Turning the Bed (and Bedroom) into a Trigger for Sleep

Another way to establish a strong foundation for sleep is to make sure your bed and bedroom become triggers or cues for sleep. Over time, if you spend a lot of time in your bed or bedroom doing work or any other intellectually stimulating activities, having arguments or important discussions, exercising, and so on, you can develop what sleep researchers call *conditioned arousal*.

Conditioned arousal means that your brain has learned to associate being in bed with being alert and awake. Sounds like the opposite of what you need, right? Well, it is. In order to improve your sleep, you might have to teach your brain something new—that the bed and bedroom are places for sleep. How do you do this? It's simple but not easy. Basically, you have to avoid doing anything other than sleeping (or sexual activity) in your bed. We have included some quick tips below. Sleep experts refer to many of these strategies as *stimulus control strategies*, as they help you change the bed from a stimulus or cue for being awake into a stimulus or cue for sleeping. Try them out over the next week, and check off the ones you've tried.

- Make the bed and bedroom a relaxing, calming sanctuary for sleep.

- Avoid using any electronic devices in bed.

- Keep your electronic devices in another room so that you're not tempted to use them in bed.

- Avoid significant conversations, phone calls, or work in bed.

- Get out of bed quickly after your alarm goes off or after you wake up.

- Avoid pressing the snooze button, as doing so will simply teach your brain that the bed is a place in which to wake up repeatedly.

- Avoid spending time in bed during the day. Do not make your bed a place to hang out and relax when you're awake.

- Try not to have a home office in your bedroom. If this is not possible, cordon off a separate area that is specifically for work.

- Reading is okay as part of your bedtime routine, but limit it to a few minutes before you go to sleep.

- Avoid watching television in your bed or bedroom (unless it's part of your bedtime routine and helps you sleep).

- Avoid staying in bed for long periods trying to get to sleep or worrying about the fact that you can't sleep.

- If you awaken in the night and can't get back to sleep within fifteen to thirty minutes, get out of bed, go to another room, and engage in a quiet, relaxing activity. Return to bed when you start to feel sleepy.

These strategies will also help you to increase your *sleep efficiency*. Sleep efficiency is the proportion of time spent in bed that you're asleep. If, for example, you spend ten hours in bed, and eight of those hours are spent sleeping, you would have a sleep efficiency of 80 percent (8/10 x 100). If your sleep efficiency is much below 70 percent, you probably need to work on spending less time in bed. On the other hand, if your sleep efficiency is very high (90 percent to 95 percent), and you fall asleep as soon as your head hits the pillow, you might be sleep deprived. This is because it is normal, on average, to take about thirty minutes to fall asleep. People who fall asleep in less than ten minutes might not be getting enough sleep. Consider making your bedtime a little earlier or your wake-up time a little bit later (by, perhaps, around fifteen to thirty minutes), and see what happens.

Moving Forward

People with PTSD commonly struggle with sleep. Correcting your sleep is no small task; however, it is an important one. In this chapter, we have reviewed several strategies you can use to establish a strong foundation of healthy sleep habits. One important step is to develop a consistent sleep schedule that works for you and matches well with your circadian clock. The most important aspect of a sleep schedule is that you have a consistent time at which you get out of bed every morning. Remember that your rise time will help to set your sleep time later on. Try to maximize the amount of sleep drive that you accumulate throughout the day by avoiding naps and excessive caffeine and by staying relatively active. Don't compensate for a poor night's sleep by going to bed particularly early, sleeping in, napping, or reducing your daytime activity. Avoiding stimulating activities in your bedroom will help ensure that your brain associates the bed and bedroom only with sleep. Over time, you will probably find that the bedroom becomes a place associated with sleepiness, calmness, and relaxation. Try to maximize your sleep efficiency by making sure that you're sleeping for most of the time when you're in bed. As your sleep improves, you might also find that your mood, energy level, and PTSD symptoms also improve. You're likely to be less reactive to stressors and more able to use many of the other coping strategies we have talked about in this book. In the next chapter, we discuss ways to manage a specific sleep problem associated with PTSD—nightmares.

CHAPTER 9

Taking Control Back from Your Nightmares

In the previous chapter, we told you that sleep problems are common among people with PTSD. One reason for this is that many people with PTSD have nightmares. In fact, studies have found that around 60 to 70 percent of people with PTSD experience nightmares (Kilpatrick et al. 1997; Schreuder, Kleijn, and Rooijmans 2000). Nightmares can take many forms. Some people have nightmares that wake them up immediately. Others have scary dreams that they remember only when they wake up the next morning. The nightmare may be an exact depiction of your traumatic event that is replayed over and over again, or it may just have elements that are related to it in some way. You may also have nightmares about only one part of the traumatic event. Regardless of how you experience nightmares, they can cause a lot of problems.

Nightmares can interfere with the quality of your sleep, especially when they wake you up, and they make it difficult for you to fall back to sleep again. Nightmares tend to occur early in your sleep cycle (Davis 2009). So when a nightmare wakes you up, it prevents you from getting into the restorative stages of slow-wave sleep. This can start a vicious cycle. With a lack of sleep or low-quality sleep, you are likely going to be emotionally vulnerable the next day and be more susceptible to experiencing bodily arousal and emotional distress. You may also be more reactive to PTSD triggers or less able to cope with your symptoms. As you get closer to your bedtime, you may start to become anxious about going to sleep, fearing another nightmare. So, you may put off going to sleep by watching television or doing something else to keep yourself up (such as drinking coffee), which then will have an even further negative impact on your sleep. When you finally do fall asleep, these things may leave you more susceptible to nightmares. And thus the cycle keeps going, and it may even gain momentum (Davis 2009). Given this, you would probably not be surprised to learn that, in addition to sleep problems, nightmares can lead to increased emotional distress and worse physical health when you have PTSD (Clum, Nishith, and Resick 2001; Krakow et al. 2002).

Unfortunately, nightmares can be difficult to address, and even when people get psychological treatment for PTSD, nightmares don't always go away (Spoormaker and Montgomery 2008). Because of this, some mental health professionals have begun to develop specialized cognitive-behavioral treatments that focus exclusively on helping people with nightmares. One such treatment is imagery rehearsal therapy (Krakow and Zadra 2010).

Imagery rehearsal therapy is a brief treatment (just four sessions), and the goal is for you to actively change a nightmare or unpleasant dream into a new dream. Basically, you take the nightmare that you frequently have and change it in any way that you want. You can change the outcome. You can incorporate more positive imagery. You can change actions that you or other people take in the dream. You can even create an entirely new dream. You can do whatever feels right to you. Then you regularly rehearse the new dream. Imaging the new dream while awake is thought to influence the content of your dreams. So, over time, your nightmares become less powerful, reduce in frequency, or change over into your new, less upsetting dreams. Sounds too simple, right? Maybe, but a number of studies have shown that this approach can reduce the number of nightmares people have, as well as the amount of distress that they have about their nightmares (Krakow and Zadra 2010; Moore and Krakow 2010). This chapter will take you through some skills from imagery rehearsal therapy (Krakow 2002; Krakow and Zadra 2010) to help you manage your nightmares.

Tracking Your Nightmares

Before we get into rewriting your nightmares, it can be a good idea to monitor your nightmares. This will give you a better idea of how often you have nightmares and what types you have. It can also help you identify connections between stress during the day and your vulnerability to have nightmares when you go to bed. Exercise 9.1 is designed to help you with this. Before you go to bed, rate how stressful your day was on a scale from 0 (not stress at all) to 10 (an incredibly stressful day). Next, rate whether you have any fears about going to sleep on a scale from 0 (no fear at all) to 10 (a high level of fear). Then go to bed. When you wake up in the morning, write down how many hours you slept and whether you had any nightmares. Rate any nightmares you had on a scale from 0 (not upsetting at all) to 10 (very upsetting). Then take a moment to think about the content of the nightmares. You don't need to pore over all the details of the nightmare; instead, just think about whether the nightmare was a close depiction of your traumatic event (Replay) or just had elements of it—that is, the nightmare was about something completely different, but some images or experiences from your traumatic event crept into the nightmare (Related). It may also be that you had a nightmare or unpleasant dream that wasn't related to your traumatic event at all (Unrelated). Finally, indicate whether the nightmare woke you up. If you remember, you can also write in how long it took you to fall back to sleep.

Exercise 9.1. Monitoring Your Nightmares

Day	Stress During the Day (0–10)	Fear About Going to Sleep (0–10)	Total Hours You Slept	How Many Nightmares	How Upsetting Nightmares Were (0–10)	Type of Nightmare	Did Nightmare Wake You Up?
Monday						Replay ___ Related ___ Unrelated ___	
Tuesday						Replay ___ Related ___ Unrelated ___	
Wednesday						Replay ___ Related ___ Unrelated ___	
Thursday						Replay ___ Related ___ Unrelated ___	

Day	Stress During the Day (0–10)	Fear About Going to Sleep (0–10)	Total Hours You Slept	How Many Nightmares	How Upsetting Nightmares Were (0–10)	Type of Nightmare	Did Nightmare Wake You Up?
Friday						Replay _____ Related _____ Unrelated _____	
Saturday						Replay _____ Related _____ Unrelated _____	
Sunday						Replay _____ Related _____ Unrelated _____	

If you experience a number of different nightmares during the week, it may be helpful to jot down a few words that describe each nightmare. This can help you keep better track of which nightmares are more unpleasant than others and which tend to occur more frequently. It will also help you choose a nightmare that you would like to rewrite. Finally, examining your nightmares can help you think about whether any of them touch upon any of your negative beliefs or stuck points that you identified in chapter 4. For example, does the nightmare bring up concerns about your safety or the safety of others? Maybe your nightmare touches on issues of trust and intimacy or on concerns about not having power or control. These are all important things to be aware of. First, it may bring to light some stuck points that need a little more attention. Second, this information can help give you some idea of what you may want to focus on in rewriting your nightmare.

Selecting Your Nightmare

The first step in rewriting your nightmare or unpleasant dream is identifying one that you would like to change (Krakow 2002; Krakow and Zadra 2010). You have a couple of options here. You could start by focusing on your most upsetting dream or a nightmare that is a replay of your traumatic event. However, this is often discouraged in imagery rehearsal therapy (Krakow and Zadra 2010). Those kinds of nightmares may bring up a lot of intense and unpleasant emotions, and revisiting them may also cause intrusive thoughts and memories. This can interfere with your ability to create and rehearse a new dream in your imagination. The goal here is to help you learn the process of changing nightmares into new dreams and then rehearsing those dreams. We want you to have some initial success with that goal and become familiar with this process. Once you feel comfortable with this process, you can gradually move on to the more upsetting dreams that you have—just as in chapter 5 you began exposure exercises slowly, gradually approaching things that you fear. It is kind of like learning how to drive. You didn't have your first driving lessons on the highway during rush hour. Instead, you started out slowly, driving around an empty parking lot or down an empty street. Once you got more comfortable and familiar with the car, you slowly moved on to more challenging streets. That's the approach we are taking here. So once you've identified a nightmare or unpleasant dream that you would feel comfortable working with, you can move on to writing about it (Krakow 2002).

Once you have a nightmare in mind, take out a sheet of paper and write a description of it from start to finish. As you write, imagine that the event is happening right now and use "I" statements (for example, *I am driving in my car on the highway. The radio is playing, and my favorite song is on.*). You don't need to worry about punctuation or spelling, and you don't need to go into tremendous detail. You want to end up with a short story of your nightmare (Krakow 2002).

If you noticed that this exercise brought up any unpleasant emotions, thoughts, or memories about your traumatic event, you may want to take a break before you move on to the next exercise and use some of the skills you learned earlier to address these feelings. For example, you may want to pair this exercise with distraction strategies (chapters 2, 6, and 7) or grounding skills (chapter 2). You could also use progressive muscle relaxation or some other skills for anxiety (chapter 3). Particular emotion regulation skills may also be helpful, such as self-soothing (chapter 6), or skills specifically focused on dealing with intrusive thoughts, such as mindfulness or cognitive defusion (chapter 4).

Changing the Nightmare

Once you are ready, you can begin working on rewriting the nightmare. The instructions here are quite simple. Take out another sheet of paper. As with the previous exercise, you want to write a short story of your new dream as though it is happening right now and use "I" statements (Krakow 2002). In writing your new dream, you are in complete control and can change the nightmare in any way you want. You don't need to change it into something positive. You don't have to change the entire thing—you can change just one part of it. For example, you might decide that you just want to change the end of the nightmare. Or you may decide that you want to change the whole thing. You can suspend all reality and do anything you want or have anything happen in your new dream (Krakow 2002; Krakow and Zadra 2010). As we mentioned earlier, in writing your new dream, you may also want to think about modifying your dream in ways that address your stuck points (for example, powerlessness, helplessness, or self-blame) that you identified in chapter 4, especially if situations related to those stuck points regularly come up in your nightmare. Alternatively, you may want to think about different choices you could make or actions you could take that might affect the outcome of your nightmare. You also don't have to do any of that. In imagery rehearsal therapy, you can change your nightmare in any way that feels right to you (Krakow 2002; Krakow and Zadra 2010).

Once you have a new dream written, read it out loud to yourself. If there are any other ideas that come to mind while reading, go ahead and fold those into your story. When you are done, you want to take a minute to assess what the experience was like for you (Krakow 2002). You can ask yourself the following questions:

- What was this exercise like for you?

- Did you notice a difference in how you felt writing about your nightmare versus writing about your new dream?

- How do you feel about your new dream?

- What kind of thoughts or emotions does it bring up?

Taking control of your nightmare can be an empowering exercise. It can remind you that you are in the driver's seat when it comes to your PTSD symptoms.

Rehearsing Your New Dream

Now that you have your new dream, you want to become familiar with it. Imagery rehearsal therapy offers some tips on how you can do this (Krakow 2002; Krakow and Zadra 2010). You want to rehearse your new dream at least once per day and for at least a few minutes, although it is best if you do it for ten to twenty minutes. To rehearse your new dream, find a quiet space away from distractions. You want to make sure you can focus all of your attention on it. Read over your new dream and visualize in your mind everything that happens in it. Some of the mindfulness skills you learned in previous chapters may help with this. Try to make the images as vivid as possible. Really connect with your dream, even imagining what it would feel like to be in your dream—what would you smell, what would you feel, what would you see, what would you hear? As you become more familiar with the dream, you may find that you no longer need to read over your new dream story to bring it to mind. Although we want you to rehearse your new dream at least once a day, initially it may be better to rehearse it a couple of times a day. Some clinicians also advise that you rehearse your new dream before you go to bed at night, followed by a relaxation exercise, such as progressive muscle relaxation or deep breathing (Davis 2009).

As you progress in rehearsing your new dream, if new imagery comes up that you would like to incorporate into your new dream, feel free to do that. You can change your new dream anytime that you want. Then, once you feel ready, you can move on to another nightmare or unpleasant dream. It is completely up to you when you move on to another nightmare. You can even work on more than one nightmare at a time; however, in imagery rehearsal therapy, it is recommended that you work on only one or two nightmares per week (Krakow and Zadra 2010).

Monitoring Your Progress

Once you start rehearsing your new dream, it can be a good idea to monitor how your sleep, nightmares, and fears about going to sleep change over time. If you aren't noticing any changes, you may want to increase the amount of time you spend rehearsing the new dream. You may also want to make some additional modifications to the new dream or focus on a different nightmare or unpleasant dream. It may also be a sign that you need to continue to combine dream rehearsal with other skills mentioned in this book, such as emotion regulation skills, mindfulness, or exposure. Fill out the monitoring form in exercise 9.2 when you wake up in the morning.

Exercise 9.2. Monitoring Changes in Your Sleep, Nightmares, and Fears About Going to Sleep

Day	How Many Times Did You Rehearse Your New Dream?	On Average, How Long Was Each Rehearsal Session?	How Many Hours Did You Sleep?	Did You Have Any Nightmares?	How Upsetting Were Those Nightmares? (0–10)	Did the Nightmares Wake You Up?	How Much Fear Did You Have About Going to Sleep (0–10)?
Monday							
Tuesday							
Wednesday							
Thursday							
Friday							
Saturday							
Sunday							

A Few Important Points

As you start the process of taking back control from your nightmares using these techniques, there are a couple of points that you should remember.

- If you have trouble remembering your nightmares or if your nightmares are vague, that's okay. The focus of this technique is really on creating a new dream, not connecting with or delving into your nightmare. Therefore, even if you remember only a small piece of your nightmare, you can use that piece to create a new dream.

- If you only have one nightmare, and it is too painful to approach, just create a dream that you would like to have and rehearse that (Krakow 2002). Remember, your new dream can be anything that feels right to you—it doesn't have to be about your traumatic event. It can be anything you want it to be.

- People differ in their ability to bring images to mind and connect with those images. Therefore, you may want to also practice just imagining pleasant experiences in your life. Try to bring to mind an experience that is vivid and positive for you. Try to connect with what emotions you were experiencing. Instead of verbally describing the scene, practice bringing to mind what you saw. What colors did you see? Were there other people around? What were they wearing? What sounds did you hear? Try to connect with all of your senses and to experience the situation as though you have gone back in time and are right there. Or, if revisiting the past feels uncomfortable to you, you can imagine what you would like your life to look like in the future. You can also simply close your eyes and try to recreate your environment in your mind.

- Remember, these exercises have you bring up thoughts or images that may be connected to your traumatic event. Therefore, you should plan ahead and have an idea as to what coping strategies you can use should you start to experience intrusive thoughts or unpleasant emotions.

Moving Forward

Nightmares are quite common among people with PTSD, and they can be difficult to tackle. You may find that some of the skills presented earlier in this book, such as exposure, emotion regulation strategies, or strategies for coping with intrusive thoughts, lead you to have fewer nightmares. You may also find that you have to use a number of different strategies, including the techniques discussed in this chapter, to deal with your nightmares. That's okay. You can approach many of the symptoms of PTSD from a number of different angles. Using the techniques discussed in this chapter to manage your nightmares may be just one part of the puzzle. If you have unhealthy sleep habits, or if you are not effectively dealing with stress during the day, these things can increase the likelihood that you will have nightmares. Therefore, you want to make sure you are taking steps to improve your sleep, using the strategies discussed in chapter 8. Finding ways to manage the stress and anxiety you feel during the day, such as by revisiting the skills in chapter 3, will also help you manage your nightmares. The next chapter in this book may also help with stress and anxiety, as it is focused on increasing positive emotions and building a fulfilling and meaningful life.

CHAPTER 10

Skills to Increase Positive Emotions and Well-Being

As we mentioned in chapter 1, people with PTSD may experience symptoms that look a lot like depression. Some may not find pleasure in activities that they used to enjoy; they can have difficulty experiencing positive emotions, such as joy and happiness; and sometimes they feel detached from people in their lives. This group of symptoms is often referred to as *emotional numbing*. Some people with PTSD even describe the experience as feeling like a wall has been built that blocks positive (but definitely not negative) emotions. Other symptoms associated with PTSD can make these symptoms worse. For example, dissociation can make it hard to feel the full spectrum of emotions, positive or negative. Constantly being hyperaroused or hypervigilant to threat or danger will make it difficult to notice the good things in life and to connect with positive emotions. In addition, as mentioned in earlier chapters, avoidance of people, places, or situations can limit opportunities to engage in activities that give you a sense of happiness and well-being. In addition, some people with PTSD suffer from depression as well, which interferes greatly with the experience of pleasure (Perkonigg et al. 2000).

When you're in a lot of pain, it can be easy to focus mainly on ways to reduce symptoms or relieve suffering. In fact, much of this book is devoted to ways to do just that. At the same time, it can be just as helpful to work on increasing positive experiences and emotions, which can breathe energy into your everyday life. Building the positive aspects of your life and feeling happier more often can also protect you against the effects of stress. It's much easier to weather stressful events when you have something positive to fall back on. Moreover, working on this can go a long way in reducing depression and other emotional difficulties (Dobson et al. 2008; Seligman, Rashid, and Parks 2006; Sin and Lyubormirsky 2009).

Fortunately, cognitive-behavioral strategies and skills can help you get in touch with positive emotions and build positive experiences into your daily life. We will cover several of these strategies in this chapter. You will probably notice that all of the strategies we discuss have one important thing in common: the most effective methods all involve *taking action*. In fact, one of the more useful behavioral treatments for these symptoms is called *behavioral activation*, and some clinicians have begun to combine cognitive-behavioral treatments for PTSD and behavioral activation with good results (Gros et al. 2012; Strachan et al. 2012). Many of the skills that we discuss in this chapter are consistent with behavioral activation and focus on the basic idea that to experience something different, such as more happiness or well-being, you often have to do something different.

Practice Mindfulness of Pleasant Events

In your efforts to build positive emotions into your life, an important first step is to begin to mindfully pay attention to positive or pleasant experiences. If you struggle with PTSD and related problems (such as depression), you might have gotten used to doing the opposite—paying close attention to and looking out for negative events. Remember when we discussed hypervigilance to threats as a core symptom of PTSD? Well, if you're looking out for frightening or depressing things that might happen, it will be difficult to notice the good things in your life. Imagine you are walking through a rose garden. Your primary goal is to avoid being stung by a bee or wasp or pricked by a thorn. With that goal, what do you notice as you walk through that garden? It's likely that you will be keenly aware of any buzzing sounds, the sensation of things landing on you, and the locations of all the thorns that could prick you. You might not even notice the beautiful flower arrangements, because you're looking out for danger. Try out exercise 10.1 to learn a bit about how your attention works. From what we know about attention, we tend to see what we're looking for.

Exercise 10.1. Finding What You're Looking For

Look around wherever you are, and try to find as many *green things* as you possibly can. Now, in the space below, write down all of the green things that you noticed:

_____

_____

_____

_____

Now, close your eyes and try to remember all of the brown, blue, or yellow things that you noticed. Write these down below:

_____

_____

_____

_____

Most of us will find that we don't remember very many brown, blue, or yellow things at all. This is because we were not looking for them. For another brief exercise in awareness, watch the YouTube video "Test Your Awareness: Do the Test" (https://m.youtube.com/watch?v= Ahg6q cgoay4).

Being mindful of pleasant events involves paying close attention to the roses. In chapter 3, we described how you can use mindfulness to cope with the symptoms of anxiety. Well, you can also use mindfulness to get in touch with positive emotions. Mindfulness is the act of paying close attention to something that is happening in the here and now. It involves having your mind open to your experience, right now. When you practice mindfulness, you are as alert and awake as a frog waiting for the next fly to come by. Your mind is in the present, and you gently let go of worries about the future or distress about the past. You pay attention to your experiences without trying to change them, escape them, or hold onto them. This is not easy to do.

When we pay attention to our experiences in the present moment, we often want to escape some of these experiences (those that are negative or painful) and hold onto others (the happy or positive ones). When practicing mindfulness, do your best to let go of these efforts to change or filter what is happening around you; allow yourself to simply experience it all.

When trying to mindfully focus on the present moment, our minds will sometimes stray and get caught up in memories, plans, worries, judgments, and so on. This is common; don't worry if you find it happening. Simply bring your attention back to the present whenever your mind strays. If you find your mind straying again, just continue to gently bring it back to your experiences in the here and now. Staying in the present will get easier with regular practice.

Attend to Pleasant Events Right Now

One way to mindfully attend to pleasant events is simply to do something you like and pay close attention to your experiences. Lose yourself in what you are doing, and let go of thoughts of the past or future. Just experience the activity right now. You may or may not feel any positive emotion. That's okay; don't try to make yourself feel anything, and avoid checking whether you feel happy. Doing so will take you out of the experience. Even if you're simply going for a short walk, walk down the street or along the trail with your eyes wide open, and absorb all that you see and smell and feel around you. Keep your ears open for sounds. Do your best to notice any beauty or pleasant experiences, even if these things seem trivial or unimportant. There are many ways to practice mindfulness of positive experiences:

- Make or purchase one of your favorite hot beverages. Pay close attention to how the cup feels in your hand, the odor emanating from the beverage, and your desire to drink it. Bring it close to your mouth, and notice if the sensations you experience change. Do you notice steam rising from the cup and warmth on your lips or face? Has the smell of the beverage become stronger? Are you feeling any keen anticipation of drinking it? Pay mindful attention to these things, with an open and curious mind. Take a sip, and notice all of the sensations you experience. Notice if you feel any pleasurable sensations or enjoyment (it's okay if you don't).

- Go for a walk in an area that you like. Pay attention to your surroundings. Notice the feeling of the air or wind on your face or arms, any sounds that you hear, and all of the sights around you. Turn on your "positive-events radar" by actively looking for things that you might like or enjoy—the birds in the trees, the children laughing or playing, the color of the grass, the sound of water or rustling leaves, and so on. Pay close attention to all of these experiences. Also try to notice any sensations of happiness or pleasure that you feel.

- Spend time with someone you feel close to. Really throw your mind into simply being with this person. If you're having a conversation, keep your mind completely focused on the conversation. Notice what it feels like to be with this person who is so important to you. Pay attention to that person. What is she wearing? What facial expressions is she making? How close is she to you? If your mind strays to worries or plans, memories or concerns, gently guide your attention back to the experience of being with this person.

These pleasant activities listed are only examples. You can choose any activity that works for you. The goal is simply to get practice at being mindful of pleasant or positive experiences. The next step is to describe them. Use exercise 10.2 to do this. Write a detailed description of your experiences. Be sure to include any and all pleasant aspects of them, including your emotions, sensations, positive thoughts, sounds, smells, sights, and so on. Although the main skill we're suggesting in this section has to do with paying attention to positive experiences when they happen, writing these experiences down can also be valuable. As you write down your positive experiences, you might notice that positive emotions arise. Also, if you write down your experiences, you might be more likely to remember them, and they will be there for you to go back and review later on. Therefore, in addition to completing exercise 10.2, you might consider keeping a diary to keep track of the particularly enjoyable experiences you've had each day.

Exercise 10.2. Mindfully Describe Pleasant Events

_____

_____

_____

_____

_____

_____

_____

_____

Actively Search for Sources of Positive Emotion in Your Daily Life

Another way to connect with positive emotions is to search for the sources of such emotions in your daily life. Imagine you're a surveyor trying to find water sources in a desert. You survey the geography of the area, determine where the plants seem to be growing, examine the dips and rises in the landscape, and use equipment to find the best sources of water. Sometimes you notice the shimmer of water in the distance, but when you get closer, you realize that it was just a mirage. At other times, you might turn a corner and discover water where you least expected it.

Similarly, to figure out what you can do to build positive emotions, start by surveying your life and figuring out which of your activities are related to positive emotions. Much like searching for water in the desert, however, you might sometimes encounter mirages—activities you think are pleasurable that actually are not. At other times, you might think the landscape is barren, but in fact, there's a source of water right underneath your feet. Before you carefully survey your daily life, you might think that you don't experience any pleasure. Do your best to search for positive experiences with an open mind and a sense of curiosity and discovery. For the last sentence of each section below, there is a blank space in which you can write another positive feeling that you might experience.

Exercise 10.3. Positive Experiences

1. To get warmed up with this, complete the sentences below about the past week. The prompts cover a variety of positive feelings: enjoyment, happiness, excitement, peacefulness, capability, and confidence.

   This week, I really enjoyed _____.

   This week, I felt happy when _____.

   This week, I felt excited when _____.

   This week, I felt peaceful when _____.

   This week, I felt capable when _____.

   This week, I felt confident when _____.

   This week, I felt _____ when _____.

2. Now, complete the sentences below, thinking of how you feel in general when you do certain activities.

   When I _____, I feel happy.

   When I _____, I feel excited.

   When I _____, I feel peace.

   When I _____, I feel capable.

   When I _____, I feel confident.

   When I _____, I feel _____.

3. It can also be helpful to reconnect to activities you used to enjoy.

In the past, I really enjoyed _____.

In the past, doing _____ made me feel confident and capable.

In the past, when I _____, I felt _____.

4. Finally, think of positive or enjoyable activities you might be doing if you were not struggling quite as much with PTSD or related problems.

If I wasn't struggling so much, I would really like to _____

_____

_____.

    If you had difficulty completing some of the sentences above, that's okay; you've still gotten off to a good start. If you're depressed, you might find that you look at things with a negative bias. You find it easier to think of times when you felt incompetent and unhappy. The good news is that focusing on events related to positive emotions will help chip away at that negative bias. There are two ways to pan for gold. You can spend your time looking for pebbles of ordinary rock, or you can spend your time looking for gold nuggets. Which strategy do you think would get you the most gold?

Build Positive Activities into Your Daily Life

Another important step is to start building positive experiences into your daily life. Take what you learned in the survey above, and start putting together a list of activities to add to your daily life. In exercise 10.4, try to come up with at least ten positive activities that you could engage in on a regular basis.

Exercise 10.4. My List of Positive Activities

_____

_____

_____

_____

_____

_____

_____

_____

_____

_____

This list is just a start. It is also helpful to consult a longer list of possible activities. Table 10.1 below is a list of activities that might be pleasurable or that might give you a sense of accomplishment or mastery (because doing things that make you feel capable and skilled is itself enjoyable, and it can also provide a buffer against feelings of stress and can improve your daily life). We have kept this list short and primarily included activities that are brief and probably easy to do in the course of your day. For a more extensive list, you may wish to look at the _Pleasant Events Schedule_, developed by Dr. Peter Lewinsohn (http://www.healthnetsolutions.com/dsp/pleasant eventsschedule.pdf) or the list of pleasant events in Dr. Marsha Linehan's _Dialectical Behavior Therapy Skills Training Manual_ (Linehan 2015).

Review the list below in table 10.1, and circle activities that could work for you. Note that, at first, you might find that you do not enjoy these activities or get any sense of mastery or accomplishment from them. That's okay. Often our emotions and moods can take longer to change.

Table 10.1. List of Possible Positive Activities

Activities That Might Be Pleasant or Enjoyable	Activities That Might Give You a Sense of Accomplishment or Mastery
Eating a good meal, snack, or special treat	Doing laundry, vacuuming, or other housework
Enjoying your favorite hot beverage	Spending time working on an important task
Cooking or preparing a meal or snack	Washing your car or organizing and tidying a room
Lying down, resting, or napping	Working on a puzzle or challenging game
Exercising, stretching, or doing yoga	Standing up for your feelings, wishes, or needs
Receiving a massage, or massaging yourself	Fixing or building something
Hugging or being close to someone physically	Taking care of bills or finances
Playing with children	Creating or organizing a to-do list
Talking with a good friend or loved one	Reading a challenging book
Engaging in sexual activity	Working on or completing a writing project
Playing a game with someone	Doing some research on jobs or volunteer work
Spending time on your electronic device	Doing volunteer work, helping others
Sitting or walking outside and viewing nature	Cooking a new or challenging meal
Looking at art	Solving a daily life problem of some kind

Activities That Might Be Pleasant or Enjoyable	Activities That Might Give You a Sense of Accomplishment or Mastery
Spending time with a pet	Practicing music, martial arts, or another skill
Reading a book, poetry, the newspaper, or an article	Learning a new computer application or operating system
Writing a blog, diary, journal, or poetry	Working on goals for personal growth or therapy
Creating art, painting, doodling, or drawing	Doing something you've been avoiding
Listening to music or sounds of nature	Trying something new or a little scary
Singing, dancing, laughing, or smiling	Helping someone with homework or another difficult task
Engaging in your religious or spiritual practice	Organizing an event, party, or celebration
Complimenting or doing something nice for someone	Teaching someone how to do something
Taking care of an animal or pet	Working on health or financial goals

Using the list in table 10.1 (or your own list of activities), schedule yourself to do at least two positive activities and at least two mastery activities each day, using the form in exercise 10.5. If you need to, start slowly—with activities that you think will be easier to accomplish—and build from there. We have included rows for three of each type of activity, in case you decide to do more than two. In the second column, write the time when you plan to do the activity. Describe the activity you have planned in the third column. And in the last column, describe what you actually did and include a rating for the feelings of pleasure and mastery you gained from the activity. Use a scale from 0 to 5, with 0 being no pleasure or mastery and 5 being intense enjoyment or mastery. For example, if your pleasure rating was 3 and your mastery rating was 1, you would write "P = 3, M = 1" next to the activity that you did. We have included an example in the form.

Exercise 10.5. Daily Schedule of Positive Activities

Day: Monday

Activity	Time	Activity Scheduled (Describe what you planned)	What I Did (Describe what you did)
Example	7 a.m.	Walk dog	Walked dog. M = 1, P = 3
Positive Activity 1			
Positive Activity 2			
Positive Activity 3			
Mastery Activity 1			
Mastery Activity 2			
Mastery Activity 3			

Reflect on Pleasant Events

We hope that, by this point in the chapter, you have begun to practice mindfulness of positive activities and have gotten your feet wet with building these activities into your everyday life. Another helpful strategy is to remember and reflect on positive events regularly. Most of us spend a fair amount of time rehashing and remembering unpleasant events. This makes sense. When something bad happens, it's possible that if we really think about it, we might be able to prevent it from happening again. The problem is that our brains are designed to remember things that we repeatedly encounter or think about—you're more likely to remember a telephone number if you use it regularly than if you just write it down once. What do you think will happen, then, if you spend more time thinking about unpleasant events than you do thinking about pleasant ones? We suggest that you try to reverse this pattern of focusing on the bad things that happen, and get some practice reflecting on and thinking about pleasant events. The pioneers of *positive psychology*, Dr. Martin Seligman and others, have developed a simple and effective way to reflect on positive events (Seligman et al. 2005). This is called the *Three Good Things Exercise*. This exercise has three steps:

1. Each night, before you go to sleep, think about good things that happened to you that day. These don't have to be earth-shattering life events. You might, for example, simply remember a really enjoyable cup of coffee. Or you might remember the sound of your child's voice when she or he excitedly greeted you at the door. Perhaps you did a favor for someone or did a great job on a task at work. Perhaps someone else did something nice for you or gave you a compliment. Maybe you just enjoyed a few quiet moments sitting outside. It really doesn't matter how significant or mundane the event was. Anything goes. See if you can come up with three of these positive events.

2. Next, write down these events, describing exactly what happened, how you felt, and what was positive or enjoyable about each of them.

3. The third step is to think about *why* each of these positive events happened. For example, let's say one of your pleasant events was a great conversation with a friend about your weekend. In step 3, you might write something like, "I really enjoyed talking with Sally yesterday. We had a great time talking about our weekends. One reason it was so great was that Sally was really interested in what I had to say. We have such great conversations because we are kindred spirits, and we really care about each other."

Often considered the most important step, the last step requires you to really examine and analyze the positive events that have happened to you. When you think a lot about the positive events that happened to you, these events can become burned into your brain. As a result, you're more likely to remember them in the future. Building positive memories, just like building positive events into your life, can help increase your experience of positive emotions and happiness. Indeed, one study found that people who completed the three good things exercise every evening for one week reported increased happiness lasting for at least six months (Seligman et al. 2005). The study stopped at six months following the one-week exercise, so it's possible that the increases in happiness last longer. Try out this exercise for a week or so, and see how you like it. Many people like it so much that they end up continuing to do it every day, every few days, or at least once a week.

Building Meaningful Activities into Your Life

Another way to get in touch with positive emotions is to engage in activities that are meaningful or important to you, even if you don't immediately think of them as pleasurable. Researchers focusing on positive psychology have come up with a definition of happiness that has three parts: (a) a pleasant life, involving engagement in positive activities, (b) an engaged life, in which you are using your strengths positively, and (c) a meaningful life, which includes involvement in activities that are meaningful to you (Seligman 1998). The first couple of sections of this chapter focused mostly on the first part and a little on the second (scheduling mastery activities). In this section, we're going to focus on the third—ways to build meaningful activities into your life.

Happiness and positive emotions are not just about doing pleasant activities. Many of the activities we enjoy might spark pleasure or feelings of mastery without making us feel like what we're doing is important or meaningful. You might, for example, enjoy watching television, but do you find it an important activity? Perhaps you felt like you really accomplished something when you finished that last load of laundry, but is laundry a meaningful activity to you? If your whole life involved television and laundry, would you feel your life had meaning? The point here is that you're probably more likely to stay in touch with positive emotions if you start to build a life that involves activities that are significant to you.

The more time you spend doing activities that you find meaningful or important, the more likely you are to experience happiness and fulfillment in your everyday life. When we say, *meaningful* or *important,* we're talking about activities that fit your personal values. There are many ways to think about values, but we define *values* here as "what really matters to you" (this is consistent with the definition used in acceptance and commitment therapy; Hayes, Strosahl, and Wilson 2011). Over the past couple of decades, cognitive-behavioral therapists have begun to focus more on how to help people bring their actions in line with their values. In acceptance and commitment therapy (Hayes, Strosahl, and Wilson 2011), for example, therapists encourage their clients to use values as their compass. Values help point you in the right direction, telling you what to spend your time doing. Many of us expend great effort reducing unwanted emotions, thoughts, or sensations. But because we can never actually get rid of all the feelings we don't like, this is a losing battle. Instead, using our core values (things that are important to us) as our compass, we can move forward in much more meaningful and positive directions. This doesn't mean that unpleasant emotions won't come up. However, the more you use values to guide your choices in life, the less your unpleasant thoughts, memories, and emotions will seem like obstacles to building the life you want to live. As another example, dialectical behavior therapy (Linehan 1993a, 1993b, 2015) includes skills to help clients clarify their values and begin to take small steps to make them an active part of their everyday lives.

Clarify Your Values

The first step in increasing meaning in your everyday life is to figure out what your values are—the ideals, beliefs, and principles that are important to you. Some people's values are crystal clear, and they don't need to do any work to figure them out. But others have problems identifying their values. If you've been struggling with PTSD, it can be easy to lose sight of your values. Fortunately, there is a fairly quick way to figure out what some of your more important values might be.

For exercise 10.6, please review the list of possible values. At the bottom of the exercise, there is room to you to add other values that are important to you. Then, in the second column, rate how important this value is to you on a scale of 1 (not important at all) to 10 (extremely important). Finally, in the third column, rate how much you've acted in a way that fits that value over the past month on a scale from 1 (no effort at all) to 10 (worked extremely hard on this value). If, for example, your value is to be a loving and caring family member, how much time and effort did you put into activities that fit this value? Did you express interest in your family members' lives, provide support when it was needed, keep in contact with or visit family members you don't live with, remember birthdays, give hugs or affection, and so on?

Exercise 10.6. List of Possible Values

Possible Values	How Important Is This Value?	How Much Have You Lived This Value Over the Past Month?
Being a kind and compassionate person		
Helping others (people, animals, causes)		
Learning and discovering new things		
Contributing to my community, to society, or to the world		
Being a loving and caring family member		
Being independent		
Being committed to the work you do		
Being conscientious, well-organized, and efficient		
Having an active and healthy life		
Caring for the environment or world		
Working against injustice, inequality, cruelty, poverty, or other problems		
Other:		
Other:		
Other:		

A third way to determine your values is to think about what types of activities give you a sense of well-being or fulfillment. As an example, I came across a woman in the grocery store the other day who had a physical condition that prevented her from reaching up above her head, where the produce bags were located. When I helped her get a bag, I felt a boost in energy and a sense of warmth and happiness. I've noticed this experience on several occasions when I've helped people in small ways. As a result, I have inferred that one of my values is to be supportive and helpful to others.

A fourth way is to do the opposite: think about the things you feel guilty, ashamed, or regretful about neglecting or not doing. This can also tell us what's important to us. If you feel guilty about not keeping your place tidy, perhaps cleanliness and tidiness are important to you. Perhaps you have regretted acting harshly toward loved ones, or you felt bad for not helping someone with something just because you were tired or didn't feel like it. Those feelings might be telling you something about your values (such as being kind to loved ones or helping others). Maybe you feel sad and disappointed that you rely on others for a lot of material or emotional support. In this case, you might place value on being independent.

One important point to remember about values is that you're never really done trying to accomplish them. Values are not tasks or goals that you can simply accomplish and check off a to-do list. You don't accomplish values in the same way that you pass a test. Instead, values tell us what's important to us and light the way on our path to a meaningful, happy, and fulfilling life. Let's say, for example, that you value being a loving and caring parent. On Saturday, you spent several hours with your son, talked with him supportively about some trouble he was having with other kids at school, attended his soccer event, and played a game with him. Can you say that you've passed the "loving parent" test and can just relax and forget about it? Unfortunately not. Values are not that specific. That's the bad news. The good news is that you can almost always be doing something that fits your values. If you use values to guide your actions, you will spend a lot of time doing things that are meaningful and important to you.

Break Values into Concrete Steps and Take Action

Although values are broad and general beliefs to live by rather than items on a to-do list, you can identify specific behaviors or tasks that fit your values. And these are things that you can schedule and check off a to-do list. Doing this can help you learn to practice living according to your values. One place to start is with exercise 10.7 below. In the first column, write a value that you'd like to work on, and in the next three, write down three specific actions that fit this value. Choose specific actions that you can actually do at some point this week. Specify how often you will do them and when. As we have in the examples, underline your statement about when you will do the actions. If you use a calendar app or a physical calendar, add these actions to it on the appropriate days and times. As we mentioned earlier, if you schedule positive events, you're much more likely to do them than you are if you don't schedule them or just wait until you feel like doing them. Avoid making these decisions based on your mood. Make them based on your values and your scheduled valued activities.

Exercise 10.7. Getting from Values to Actions

Value	Specific Action 1	Specific Action 2	Specific Action 3
Be a caring and compassionate partner.	Ask Joe about his day _each day when he comes home from work._ Act interested!	Buy Joe his favorite coffee beans _when I go shopping tomorrow._	Offer to do the dishes _this evening._
Be independent and do things for myself.	Spend 30 minutes looking at job ads _on Tuesday at 10 a.m._	Spend an hour revising my résumé _on Tuesday at 1 p.m._	Come up with a plan to pay off my credit card bill _this evening after dinner._

Scheduling actions that support your values, as in exercise 10.7, can help you learn and practice living according to your values. Writing down these actions—both in a form like the one above and simply on a calendar—is also useful as a record of what you have accomplished. You can also look back at this form to see how much acting according to your values seems to be helping with your life satisfaction and your PTSD symptoms.

Breathe Value and Meaning into Your Daily Activities

Let's face it: many of the things we do on a daily basis seem relatively meaningless. We get up in the morning, go to the bathroom, eat breakfast, brush our teeth, take a shower, get ready for work or school, and so on. It might seem at times like many of the things we do are rather mundane. One way to get around this truth of everyday living is to purposely infuse daily activities with meaning.

Here's an example of how I (Alexander Chapman) do this. As a professor, I supervise many graduate and undergraduate students. Many of these students want to go on to graduate school and professional careers of various kinds, and when they apply for university, jobs, and so on, they often need recommendation letters. This most often happens in the fall, between September and December. I often find myself swamped with letters to write. Last fall it got so bad that, for about a month, most of my workday was spent writing letters. It's not like writing nice things about people is such a bad way to spend my time, but I did find it frustrating that this task was getting in the way of the many other things I needed to do. In addition, many annoying little tasks accompany writing letters of recommendation—creating online accounts for different universities where I am submitting my letters, formatting the letter appropriately, attaching my signature, converting letters to PDF format, and the list goes on.

I have discovered a great way to avoid getting bogged down and frustrated with all of these details. I remind myself of one of my most important values—to be a supportive and helpful mentor to my students. When I create my to-do list for my daily tasks, I purposely put these tasks in categories that represent my values. For example, letters go in a category "Be a supportive and helpful mentor." Whenever I look at my list of letters to write, I am reminded that all of the annoying little activities that accompany letter writing have meaning to me.

Think about regular everyday activities that don't seem meaningful to you right now. See if you can find the hidden value or meaning in these activities. Challenge yourself to actively connect seemingly mundane activities to values that are important to you. One way to do this is to take a piece of paper and write down things you normally do each day. Then, next to those things, write down a value they might relate to. Once you've done this, the next challenge is to remind yourself as you do the task that what you're doing is related to an important value. For example, if you wrote down, "Going for a walk," this action might be connected to your value of being healthy and physically fit. Whenever you go for a walk—or if you decide to take the stairs instead of an elevator or walk to the post office rather than drive—remind yourself that you're not just walking; you're working on being healthier and more physically fit. See if this changes your experience of your everyday life activities.

Important Points to Keep in Mind

As you review and try out some of the strategies in this chapter, there are a few key ideas to keep in mind. These ideas will point you in the right direction when you need guidance, help you figure out where and how to start, and remind you of what to do if you feel that you aren't doing well.

- The best way to experience positive emotions more often is to change your life from the outside in. When we feel down, depressed, or sad, many of us first try to think differently or use some kind of coping skill to reduce unwanted emotions. At other times, we might try to make ourselves feel happier by sheer force of will. Although this sometimes works, a more effective way to build positive emotions into your life is to change what you're doing. What you do has a profound effect on how you feel. How you spend your time, the people you see or spend time with, and whether you engage in positive or meaningful activities each day can have an enormous impact on your mood and emotions. In contrast, if you only do what you feel like doing, you're likely to end up with the same feelings you already have. Accordingly, most of the skills we discuss in this chapter involve changing your behavior. The following quote from Thich Nhat Hanh captures this point nicely: "Sometimes your joy is the source of your smile, but sometimes your smile can be the source of your joy."

- Start small. It can be hard to make any kind of behavioral change, whether you're trying to get out and see people more often, exercise consistently, quit smoking, get involved in a hobby, or anything. Don't set too high a goal in the beginning or try to change too much at once. When climbing a staircase, it doesn't work to try to jump twenty steps at once. There's a good chance you'll break your leg or sprain something and be unable to climb stairs for a while. If you start small, you're much more likely to be successful. If you're at the point, for example, where going out for a ten-minute walk is challenging but manageable, that's a great place to start. If you start with small activities that you can do, your success will help you build momentum, and you'll be more able to keep yourself climbing up that staircase.

- Use other skills you have learned in this book. As we mentioned earlier in this chapter, changing your behavior is often easier said than done. There are many things inside and outside of you that can get in the way of doing things that matter to you. Unpleasant thoughts and emotions can sometimes sap motivation. Time and money can also be obstacles to doing things that are important to you. If you are finding it difficult to move forward with some of these exercises, it may be helpful to identify both the internal and the external barriers to completing these exercises. Problem solving usually addresses most external barriers, but internal barriers can be more difficult to address. If you are struggling with some internal barriers, look through other chapters in this book and use some of the skills discussed in those chapters in combination with the ones discussed here.

• Start now. One of our all-time favorite quotes is the following by Alan Cohen: "Do not wait until all of the conditions are perfect for you to begin. Beginning makes the conditions perfect." Have you ever told yourself that you'll get to work once your office is completely clean? How well has that worked? Many of us have done this, and we just end up cleaning our office and never getting to our work. Or we feel overwhelmed by the thought of cleaning our office, and we end up doing nothing. If you're planning to build positive activities into your daily life, don't wait until you're happier, more energized, or less depressed to get started. If you do that, you could be waiting a long time. Instead, get started, and you'll probably find that you start feeling happier, more energized, and less depressed.

Moving Forward

To recap, PTSD symptoms can make it hard to experience pleasure and fulfillment in everyday life. Some symptoms of PTSD, such as hyperarousal, hypervigilance, and dissociation, directly interfere with your experience of pleasure and happiness. Other symptoms, such as avoidance, limit your opportunities to engage in activities that are enjoyable, meaningful, or give you a feeling of accomplishment. One of the best ways to increase positive emotions is to build those kinds of activities into your life. Consistently scheduling and engaging in these types of activities can also protect you against some of the effects of ongoing life stress. Furthermore, if you also clarify what's important to you and align your behavior with your values, your everyday life will probably start to feel more fulfilling and meaningful. Start by taking an inventory of your past and current life to discover what you enjoy doing and what gives you a sense of mastery. Then start to include more of those activities in your daily life. Clarify your values, and then be specific and concrete about things you can do that are important to you. Start small and take on only as much as you can keep up, and we're confident that you'll start to find life a lot more enjoyable and fulfilling, and that you'll be much better able to weather stress.

CHAPTER 11

Maintaining Your Recovery from PTSD

Congratulations! If you have reached this chapter, you have made it through all the other chapters in the book and are hopefully well on your way down the road to recovery from PTSD. We also hope that you have found the skills presented in these chapters to be helpful in managing the different symptoms of PTSD and that you have had some opportunities to see how these skills can help you take back control of your life from your symptoms. PTSD does not have to be a lifelong condition. Even though it may be difficult at times, there are steps you can take to lessen the severity of your symptoms and reduce the impact they have on your life. That said, just because you may feel better now doesn't mean that your work is done. Research shows that people who have recovered from PTSD may still be at higher risk for developing problems with anxiety and depression than people who have never had PTSD (Westphal et al. 2011). In addition, PTSD symptoms can come back, especially if you are exposed to another traumatic event. Therefore, it is important that you take steps to maintain your recovery from PTSD.

That's what this chapter is about—we want to make sure that all of the progress you have made up to this point is maintained and even improved upon. This chapter will give you some information on how to keep moving forward in your recovery from PTSD. This chapter will also tell you about some warning signs that might show you that you need some extra support. Finally, we'll direct you to websites that provide a wealth of information on PTSD and its treatment and that help you find people in your area who treat PTSD, should you want to go that route.

How to Maintain Your Gains

When you look back on your experience with PTSD now, you may realize that you had developed some unhealthy habits or that you feared objects, situations, or experiences that were not truly dangerous or threatening. It used to be thought that after successful treatment of PTSD, this old learning was extinguished or eliminated. However, we now know that really isn't the case. Those fears and habits don't really go away. Instead, what happened is that when you stopped giving into them, they weakened. And at the same time, you developed healthy habits and accurate beliefs, and as you strengthened them with practice, they were eventually able to compete with and override your old unhealthy habits and beliefs. However, like a muscle, without regular use and practice, these new habits can start to weaken, increasing the likelihood that some of the old ones creep back into your life. This is why it is incredibly important to view your recovery from PTSD as a lifelong process. You want to make changes in your life that allow you to maintain the progress you have made. The good news is that many of the skills we discussed in this book are good life skills in general. They are not specific to PTSD. Learning how to regulate your emotions, be more mindful, and increase your connection with activities that you find meaningful will not only keep your PTSD symptoms at bay, but will also help you build a healthy and fulfilling life.

There are a number of steps you can take to ensure that you continue to move forward in your recovery from PTSD:

- *Practice, practice, practice.* The skills discussed in this book aren't second nature. They require commitment and regular practice. Try to identify at least one coping skill to practice each week, even if you don't think that you are going to need to use it. The more you practice a coping skill, the easier it is going to be to put that skill into action when you need it.

- *Regularly revisit the different chapters in this book.* The material might seem familiar to you right now, but over time, some of this information might slip away. You want to keep it fresh in your mind. In addition, remember that when you first went over the material, you were likely in a very different place than where you are now. Rereading the material can show you how far you have come in your recovery from PTSD, and you may notice some things that you missed the first time through—skills that you did not feel ready to try at first might be helpful to you now.

- *Learn new coping skills.* Although we presented a number of skills in this book, there are many more out there. Buy some other self-help books or do some research on the Internet. You may also want to check out the PTSD Coach mobile app (http://www.ptsd.va.gov /public/materials/apps/ptsdcoach.asp). The PTSD Coach was developed by the VA's

National Center for PTSD in collaboration with the U.S. Department of Defense's National Center for Telehealth and Technology. This app is free, and you don't have to be a veteran to use it. It can provide you with information about PTSD, its symptoms, and its treatment. It also includes functions that help you identify and track your PTSD symptoms, so you can see how they change from week to week. In addition, it provides you with instructions on different ways of coping with stress. Finally, it also includes links that connect you to additional support, if you need it. It can be a useful tool in your recovery from PTSD.

- *Remind yourself of the progress you have made.* Recovering from PTSD is not an easy thing to do. Even if you are not yet exactly where you would like to be, try to compare where you are now with where you were when you started this workbook. Give yourself credit for accomplishing a major feat—facing PTSD head on and succeeding.

- *Identify or develop sources of support.* PTSD can negatively affect relationships, but social support is consistently found to protect people from the effects of a traumatic event (Agaibi and Wilson 2005). In addition to providing you with emotional support, a trusted friend or loved one can help you become more aware of early warning signs that your symptoms may be getting worse. Sometimes it can be hard to recognize when we are slipping. A trusted friend or loved one may be in a better position to recognize subtle changes in your mood or behavior that would indicate you need to take action.

- *Seek out a mental health provider (a counselor, psychologist, or psychiatrist).* After going through this workbook, you might decide that there is still some work you need to do on your PTSD symptoms. As we mentioned in chapter 1, there are a number of psychological treatments available that have been found to be successful in reducing the symptoms of PTSD. Or, even if you feel that your PTSD symptoms are no longer a problem for you, a mental health provider can still be an excellent source of support. Later on in this chapter, we will provide you with some websites that will help you identify mental health providers in your area.

- *Take action to build the life you want to live.* PTSD can make it feel as though your life is on pause or maybe even moving backward. Reducing your PTSD symptoms is the first step in your recovery. The next step is thinking about how you can build the life that you want for yourself and how you want to be in your life. Begin to identify actions that you can engage in that are consistent with these ideals. For example, if you value being compassionate and kind, there are a number of behaviors that you can engage in that are in line with that value, such as volunteering, donating money to an important cause, helping out a friend in need, or even just telling someone that you care about them.

When it comes to your life, you are in the driver's seat. No matter what thoughts, bodily sensations, or emotions you experience, you always have control over your behavior and the choices you make.

Be on the Lookout for Warning Signs

Just as you want to take steps to continue your recovery from PTSD, you also want to be aware of signs that your PTSD symptoms may be coming back or getting worse. As we said earlier, old habits and beliefs don't really go away. In some cases, they can come back rather quickly, particularly if you experience another highly stressful or traumatic event. Basically, you want to be on the lookout for negative changes in your thoughts, mood, and behavior.

Changes in Your Thoughts

Revisit chapter 4 and look at some of the negative beliefs or thoughts (that is, your stuck points) that you identified in the exercises in that chapter. Some of those thoughts might seem foreign to you now; however, at one point, you bought into them. If you start to notice some of those negative thoughts again, this could be a warning sign. In addition to these thoughts, you might notice that you are getting caught up in some of the negative thinking patterns that were identified in that chapter, such as emotional reasoning, black-or-while thinking, or catastrophizing. This could also be a warning sign that you need to attend to.

Changes in Your Mood

In addition to changes in your thoughts, you may also notice changes in your mood. For example, you might start to feel a little more reactive, on edge, and agitated. You may notice that you are worrying more often or that your mood changes rapidly. One minute you might feel fine, but a moment later, you start to feel anxious, angry, or sad. You may also find it hard to connect with positive emotions or positive emotional experiences. All of these are signs that you may be vulnerable for a slip.

Changes in Your Behavior

The top change in your behavior that you want to be on the lookout for is avoidance. In chapters 1 and 5, we talked about how avoidance is what fuels your PTSD symptoms. Therefore, you really need to be aware of moments when you start to isolate yourself from people, stop taking part in meaningful or necessary daily activities, increase behaviors aimed at trying to escape unpleasant emotions (for example, drinking more often), or simply just try to push away certain thoughts and emotions. You may also notice that your motivation has decreased or that you are having problems sleeping. These behavioral changes should be red flags that your symptoms are worsening.

In exercise 11.1, try to identify what would be warning signs that you need to look out for. Keep this list handy, and it can also be useful to share it with someone you trust. This list will help protect you by keeping you (and your loved ones) aware of potential problems, so if you do start having difficulties, you will be able to catch them early.

Exercise 11.1. Your Warning Signs

Changes in Thoughts

1. _____

_____

2. _____

_____

3. _____

_____

4. _____

_____

5. _____

_____

Changes in Mood

1. _____

_____

2. _____

_____

3. _____

_____

4. _____

_____

5. _____

_____

Changes in Behavior

1. _____

_____

2. _____

_____

3. _____

_____

4. _____

_____

5. _____

_____

If at some point you notice that you have experienced some of these changes, it doesn't mean that your PTSD symptoms are going to come back. It just means that you are vulnerable, and you should therefore take steps to address them. When you experience these symptoms, you will want to revisit some of the coping skills in this book or reach out to someone who can provide support. Basically, you want to take immediate action to ensure that these changes don't become more severe. Look back over the chapters in this book, and in exercise 11.2, write down the skills that you found to be particularly helpful for dealing with your symptoms. If you notice any warning signs down the road, you now have a list of skills that you know worked well in the past. This is going to make it easier to take action quickly and effectively.

Exercise 11.2. What You Can Do to Cope With Your Warning Signs

Coping Skills for Managing Changes in Thoughts

1. _____

_____

2. _____

_____

3. _____

_____

4. _____

_____

5. _____

_____

Coping Skills for Managing Changes in Mood

1. _____

_____

2. _____

_____

3. _____

_____

4. _____

_____

5. _____

_____

Coping Skills for Managing Changes in Behavior

1. _____

_____

2. _____

_____

3. _____

_____

4. _____

_____

5. _____

_____

Other PTSD Resources

We hope that this workbook provided you with a good amount of information on PTSD, how it develops, and how it can be dealt with. However, you may want to learn more about PTSD and its treatment. You may also want to learn more about other conditions that commonly co-occur with PTSD, such as anxiety disorders and major depression. When looking for information on the Internet, you have to be careful. You want to make sure you go to a reputable website that provides up-to-date and accurate information. Fortunately, there are a number of websites out there that do just that:

- *American Psychological Association* (http://apa.org)

  The website of the American Psychological Association can provide you with information on PTSD and other mental health disorders, as well as other mental health–related topics. Specifically, the American Psychological Association's Psychology Help Center is an online resource for consumers and includes articles that describe groundbreaking research on mental health, tips for coping with mental health problems and life stressors, and a variety of other topics that may be relevant to someone with PTSD (for example, pain, depression, and addictions). This website also includes a psychologist locator service, which you can use to search for psychologists in your area. That locator service allows you to narrow your search by the psychologists' area of specialization, gender, languages spoken, and other factors.

- *Association for Behavioral and Cognitive Therapies* (http://www.abct.org)

  Similar to the American Psychological Association website, the website for the Association for Behavioral and Cognitive Therapies offers information on mental health disorders and their treatment, including PTSD. As you can probably tell from the name of this website, this organization is focused specifically on the advancement of cognitive-behavioral treatments for different mental health disorders. This organization has also reviewed and identified numerous self-help books that provide people with coping skills that are based on current research. Books endorsed by this organization are called Self-Help Books of Merit (http://www.abct.org/shbooks/?m=mfindhelp&fa=sh_books). The website also provides helpful information on how to choose the best mental health provider, and it offers a cognitive-behavioral therapist locator service.

- *The Anxiety and Depression Association of America* (http://www.adaa.org)

  The website for the Anxiety and Depression Association of America focuses specifically on anxiety, obsessive-compulsive, mood, and trauma- and stressor-related disorders, such as PTSD. The website includes fact sheets on PTSD that describe its symptoms and

183

treatment. This website also includes free public education webinars on a variety of topics that may be relevant to someone with PTSD (for example, coping with panic attacks). Similar to the websites described above, the Anxiety and Depression Association of America website includes a therapist locator service.

- *National Institute of Mental Health* (http://www.nimh.nih.gov)

If you are particularly interested in reading more about research that is being done on PTSD, you should definitely check out the website of the National Institute of Mental Health. In addition to providing information on a number of mental health disorders, this website connects you to groundbreaking research that is being done on these disorders, including PTSD. It also tells you about exciting research that is currently being done to better understand the development of PTSD and how best to treat it.

- *U.S. Department of Veterans Affairs National Center for PTSD* (http://www.ptsd.va.gov)

If you are a veteran with PTSD, the website of the National Center for PTSD should be the first place you go. As with the other websites, this website provides basic information on PTSD and its treatment; however, it also includes a number of other helpful resources. It has articles that specifically focus on PTSD and relationships, dealing with PTSD at work or school, and PTSD and the legal system. Some of these articles are geared toward veterans with PTSD, but many are applicable to anyone with PTSD. It also includes testimonials from multiple veterans who have been diagnosed with PTSD and received treatment. This program, called *AboutFace* (http://www.ptsd.va.gov/apps/aboutface), features veterans talking about how PTSD affected their lives, how they knew they needed help, and how treatment changed their lives. You can also listen to the stories of family members who had a loved one with PTSD and those of clinicians who treat PTSD. Finally, this website offers a number of free mobile apps (including the PTSD Coach, which we described earlier) that can help you learn ways to manage your mood, be more mindful, deal with stress, and improve your parenting skills.

- *International Society for Traumatic Stress Studies* (http://www.istss.org)

This website specifically focuses on PTSD and the impact of traumatic experiences. As with the other websites, it also includes a wealth of information on why PTSD develops, its symptoms, and the best treatments currently available. It also includes a blog where top mental health professionals share current research on a variety of PTSD-relevant topics. This website also includes videos of people who share their experiences of having and receiving treatment for PTSD. This website also offers a therapist locator service.

- *International Society for the Study of Trauma and Dissociation* (http://www.isst-d.org)

This website focuses on the impact of traumatic experiences, but it is different from the ISTSS website in that it has a tremendous amount of information on dissociation. Not everyone with PTSD experiences dissociation; however, for those that do, it can be a frightening experience that is difficult to cope with. If you struggle with dissociation, this website may be able to direct you to some information or resources that will help you cope with and obtain freedom from dissociation. Like the other websites, this one offers a therapist locator service.

A Few Final Words

Before we end this workbook, we would like you to take part in one last exercise. Remember when you wrote your impact statement in chapter 4? As a reminder, in cognitive processing therapy (Resick, Monson, and Chard 2008), people write an impact statement that describes how their traumatic event changed the way they view themselves, other people, and the world. We would like you to write a new impact statement based on where you are right now. If you don't remember how to do it, the instructions are provided here. With pen and paper (since this exercise is best done handwritten), simply write your answers to the two questions in the exercise below. Try to write at least one page. You *do not* need to detail what happened during your traumatic event. Also, make sure you do this exercise when you have some privacy and the ability to sit with and express any emotions that may come up while you are writing. Don't worry about grammar, spelling, or neatness. The most important thing is that you connect with and write about your thoughts and feelings associated with your traumatic event.

Exercise 11.3. Writing an Impact Statement

1. Why do you think your traumatic event happened to you?

    _____

    _____

    _____

2. In general, how do you think your traumatic event changed the way you think about or see yourself, other people, and the world?

    _____

    _____

    _____

Now, compare your new impact statement to the impact statement you wrote way back in chapter 4. Do you notice any differences? Maybe you notice that you have fewer negative beliefs or stuck points about your traumatic event. Do you have a more balanced perspective on the world or a more compassionate view of yourself? You may also find that doing this exercise brought up fewer unpleasant emotions, such as sadness, anger, or guilt, than you experienced the first time you did it. Maybe fewer thoughts about your traumatic event came up, and those that did were less distressing.

Take a few minutes to reflect on how much you have accomplished in going through this workbook and tackling your PTSD symptoms head-on. Some of you may have noticed a major change in your symptoms, whereas others may have noticed only a few changes. PTSD can be a difficult disorder to cope with; thus, even a small change in your symptoms is something to be proud of, and it is something that you can definitely build on. It also shows that you can take action to reduce your PTSD symptoms. And, in seeing the differences in your impact statements, you have additional evidence that PTSD does not have to be a life sentence. Even though there is no way you can erase the fact that your traumatic event happened or remove the memories of that event, you have taken steps to reduce the extent to which those experiences interfere with your building the life you want to live. You are the one in control of your life, and the possibilities are endless.

References

Agaibi, C. E., and J. P. Wilson. 2005. "Trauma, PTSD, and Resilience: A Review of the Literature. *Trauma, Violence, and Abuse* 6: 195–216.

American Psychiatric Association. 2010. *Diagnostic and Statistical Manual of Mental Disorders.* 4th ed. Washington, DC: American Psychiatric Association.

American Psychiatric Association. 2013. *Diagnostic and Statistical Manual of Mental Disorders.* 5th ed. Washington, DC: American Psychiatric Association.

Asmundson, G. J., M. G. Fetzner, L. B. DeBoer, M. B. Powers, M. W. Otto, and J. A. Smits. 2013. "Let's Get Physical: A Contemporary Review of the Anxiolytic Effects of Exercise for Anxiety and Its Disorders." *Depression and Anxiety* 30: 362–73.

Babson, K. A., and M. T. Feldner. 2010. "Temporal Relations Between Sleep Problems and Both Traumatic Event Exposure and PTSD: A Critical Review of the Empirical Literature." *Journal of Anxiety Disorders* 24: 1–15.

Beck, J. S. 1995. *Cognitive Therapy: Basics and Beyond.* New York: Guilford Press.

Beckham, J. C. 1999. "Smoking and Anxiety in Combat Veterans with Chronic Posttraumatic Stress Disorder: A Review." *Journal of Psychoactive Drugs* 31: 103–10.

Brady, K. T., S. E. Back, and S. F. Coffey. 2004. "Substance Abuse and Posttraumatic Stress Disorder." *Current Directions in Psychological Science* 13: 206–9.

Breslau, N., and R. C. Kessler 2001. "The Stressor Criterion in DSM-IV Posttraumatic Stress Disorder: An Empirical Investigation." *Biological Psychiatry* 50: 699–704.

Brewerton, T. D. 2007. "Eating Disorders, Trauma, and Comorbidity: Focus on PTSD." *Eating Disorders* 15: 285–304.

Brewin, C. R., B. Andrews, and J. D. Valentine. 2000. "Meta-Analysis of Risk Factors for Posttraumatic Stress Disorder in Trauma-Exposed Adults." *Journal of Consulting and Clinical Psychology* 68: 748–66.

Burgess, A. W., and L. L. Holmstrom. 1974. "Rape Trauma Syndrome." *American Journal of Psychiatry* 131: 981–6.

Chapman, A. L., K. L. Gratz, and M. T. Tull. 2009. *The Dialectical Behavior Therapy Skills Workbook for Anxiety.* Oakland, CA: New Harbinger Publications.

Clum, G. A., P. Nishith, and P. A. Resick. 2001. "Trauma-Related Sleep Disturbances and Self-Reported Physical Health Symptoms in Treatment Seeking Female Rape Victims." *Journal of Nervous and Mental Disease* 189: 618–22.

Craske, M. G., M. Treanor, C. C. Conway, T. Zbozinek, and B. Vervliet. 2014. "Maximizing Exposure Therapy: An Inhibitory Learning Approach." *Behaviour Research and Therapy* 58: 10–23.

Davis, J. L. 2009. *Treating Post-Trauma Nightmares.* New York: Springer.

Dixon-Gordon, K. L., M. T. Tull, and K. L. Gratz. 2014. "Self-Injurious Behaviors in Posttraumatic Stress Disorder: An Examination of Potential Moderators." *Journal of Affective Disorders* 166: 359–67.

Dobson, K. S., S. D. Hollon, S. Dimidjian, K. B. Schmaling, R. J. Kohlenberg, R. Gallop, S. L. Rizvi, J. K. Gollan, D. L. Dunner, and N. S. Jacobson. 2008. "Randomized Trial of Behavioral Activation, Cognitive Therapy, and Antidepressant Medication in the Prevention of Relapse and Recurrence in Major Depression." *Journal of Consulting and Clinical Psychology* 76: 468–77.

Falsetti, S. A., and H. S. Resnick. 1997. "Frequency and Severity of Panic Attack Symptoms in a Treatment Seeking Sample of Trauma Victims." *Journal of Traumatic Stress* 10: 683–9.

Fetzner, M. G., and G. J. Asmundson. 2015. "Aerobic Exercise Reduces Symptoms of Posttraumatic Stress Disorder: A Randomized Controlled Trial." *Cognitive Behaviour Therapy* 44: 301–13.

Figueiro, M. G., B. Wood, B. Plitnick, and M. S. Rea. 2011. "The Impact of Light from Computer Monitors on Melatonin Levels in College Students." *Neuroendocrinology Letters* 32: 158–63.

Foa, E. B., E. A. Hembree, and B. O. Rothbaum. 2007. *Prolonged Exposure Therapy for PTSD.* New York: Oxford University.

Foa, E. B., and M. J. Kozak. 1986. "Emotional Processing of Fear: Exposure to Corrective Information." *Psychological Bulletin* 99: 20–35.

Grant, J. E., C. B. Donahue, and B. L. Odlaug. 2011. *Overcoming Impulse Control Problems: A Cognitive-Behavioral Therapy Program.* New York: Oxford University Press.

Gratz, K. L., and Chapman, A. L. 2009. *Freedom from Self-Harm: Overcoming Self-Injury with Skills from DBT and Other Treatments.* Oakland, CA: New Harbinger Publications.

Gros, D. F., M. Price, M. Strachan, E. K. Yuen, M. E. Milanak, and R. Acierno. 2012. "Behavioral Activation and Therapeutic Exposure: An Investigation of Relative Symptom Changes in PTSD and Depression During the Course of Integrated Behavioral Activation, Situational Exposure, and Imaginal Exposure Techniques." *Behavior Modification* 36: 580–99.

Hayes, S. C., K. D. Strosahl, and K. G. Wilson. 2011. *Acceptance and Commitment Therapy: The Process and Practice of Mindful Change.* New York: Guilford Press.

Keane, T. M., and D. H. Barlow. 2002. "Posttraumatic Stress Disorder." In *Anxiety and Its Disorders*, edited by D. H. Barlow, 418–53. 2nd ed. New York: Guilford Press.

Kessler, R. C., P. A. Berglund, O. Demler, R. Jin, K. R. Merikangas, and E. E. Walters. 2005. "Lifetime Prevalence and Age-of-Onset Distributions of DSM-IV Disorders in the National Comorbidity Survey Replication (NCS-R)." *Archives of General Psychiatry* 62: 593–602.

Kessler, R. C., A. Sonnega, E. Bromet, M. Hughes, and C. B. Nelson. 1995. "Posttraumatic Stress Disorder in the National Comorbidity Survey." *Archives of General Psychiatry* 52: 1048–60.

Kilpatrick, D. G., H. S. Resnick, J. R. Freedy, D. Pelcovitz, P. Resick, S. Roth, and B. van der Kolk. 1997. "The Posttraumatic Stress Disorder Field Trial: Evaluation of the PTSD Construct: Criteria A Through E." In *DSM-IV Sourcebook*, edited by T. A. Widiger, A. J. Frances, H. A. Pincus, M. B. First, R. Ross, and W. Davis. Vol. 4. Washington DC: American Psychiatric Press.

Koenen, K. C., and S. Galea. 2015. "Posttraumatic Stress Disorder and Chronic Disorder: Open Questions and Future Directions." *Social Psychiatry and Psychiatric Epidemiology* 50: 511–3.

Krakow, B. 2002. *Turning Nightmares into Dreams.* Audio series and treatment workbook. Albuquerque, NM: Maimonides Sleep Arts and Sciences.

Krakow, B., R. Schrader, D. Tandberg, M. Hollifield, M. P. Koss, C. L. Yau, and D. T. Cheng. 2002. "Nightmare Frequency in Sexual Assault Survivors with PTSD." *Journal of Anxiety Disorders* 16: 175–90.

Krakow, B., and A. Zadra. 2010. "Imagery Rehearsal Therapy: Principles and Practice." *Sleep Medicine Clinics* 5: 289–98.

Kripke, D. R., M. R. Marler, and E. E. Calle. 2004. "Epidemiological Health Impact." In *Sleep Deprivation: Clinical Issues, Pharmacology, and Sleep Loss Effects*, edited by E. A. Kushida, 195–210. Boca Raton, FL: Taylor and Francis.

Lejuez, C. W., D. R. Hopko, R. Acierno, S. B. Daughters, and S. L. Pagoto. 2011. "Ten Year Revision of the Brief Behavioral Activation Treatment for Depression: Revised Treatment Manual." *Behavior Modification* 35: 111–61.

Linehan, M. M. 1993a. *Cognitive-Behavioral Treatment of Borderline Personality Disorder*. New York: Guilford Press.

Linehan, M. M. 1993b. *Skills Training Manual for Treating Borderline Personality Disorder*. 1st Ed. New York: Guilford Press.

Linehan, M. M. 2015. *DBT Skills Training Manual*. 2nd Ed. New York: Guilford Press.

Litz, B. T., and L. Roemer. 1996. "Post-Traumatic Stress Disorder: An Overview." *Clinical Psychology and Psychotherapy* 3: 153–68.

Manger, T. A., and R. W. Motta. 2005. "The Impact of an Exercise Program on Posttraumatic Stress Disorder, Anxiety, and Depression." *International Journal of Emergency Mental Health* 7: 49–57.

Marshall, R. D., M. Olfson, F. Hellman, C. Blanco, M. Guardino, and E. L. Struening. 2001. "Comorbidity, Impairment, and Suicidality in Subthreshold PTSD." *American Journal of Psychiatry* 158: 1467–73.

McFarlane, A. C. 1998. "Epidemiological Evidence About the Relationship Between PTSD and Alcohol Abuse: The Nature of the Association." *Addictive Behaviors* 23: 813–25.

Moore, B. A., and B. Kraków. 2010. "Imagery Rehearsal Therapy: An Emerging Treatment for Posttraumatic Nightmares in Veterans." *Psychological Trauma: Theory, Research, Practice, and Policy* 2: 232–8.

Morin, C. M., R. R. Bootzin, D. J. Buysse, J. D. Edinger, C. A. Espie, and K. L. Lichstein. 2006. "Psychological and Behavioral Treatment of Insomnia: Update of the Recent Evidence (1998–2004)." *Sleep* 29: 1398.

Ohayon, M. M., and C. M. Shapiro. 2000. "Sleep Disturbances and Psychiatric Disorders Associated with Posttraumatic Stress Disorder in the General Population." *Comprehensive Psychiatry* 41: 469–78.

Olatunji, B. O., J. M. Cisler, and B. J. Deacon. 2010. "Efficacy of Cognitive Behavioral Therapy for Anxiety Disorders: A Review of Meta-Analytic Findings." *Psychiatric Clinics of North America* 33: 557–77.

Perkonigg, A., R. C. Kessler, S. Storz, and H. U. Wittchen. 2000. "Traumatic Events and Post-Traumatic Stress Disorder in the Community: Prevalence, Risk Factors and Comorbidity." *Acta Psychiatrica Scandinavica* 101: 46–59.

Powers, M. B., G. J. Asmundson, and J. A. Smits. 2015. "Exercise for Mood and Anxiety Disorders: The State-of-the Science." *Cognitive Behaviour Therapy* 44: 237–9.

Purdon, C. 1999. "Thought Suppression and Psychopathology." *Behaviour Research and Therapy* 37: 1029–54.

Resick, P. A., C. M. Monson, and K. M. Chard. 2008. "Cognitive Processing Therapy: Therapist's Manual." Washington, DC: U.S. Department of Veterans Affairs.

Schreuder, B. J., W. C. Kleijn, and H. G. Rooijmans. 2000. "Nocturnal Re-experiencing More Than Forty Years After War Trauma." *Journal of Traumatic Stress* 13: 453–63.

Seligman, M. E. P. 1998. "President's Column: What Is the 'Good Life'?" *APA Monitor* 29: 1.

Seligman, M. E. P., T. Rashid, and A. C. Parks. 2006. "Positive Psychotherapy." *American Psychologist* 61: 774–88.

Seligman, M. E. P., T. A. Steen, N. Park, and C. Peterson. 2005. "Positive Psychology Progress: Empirical Validation of Interventions." *American Psychologist* 60: 410–21.

Shipherd, J. C., and J. G. Beck. 2005. "The Role of Thought Suppression in Posttraumatic Stress Disorder." *Behavior Therapy* 36: 277–87.

Sin, N. L., and S. Lyubormirsky. 2009. "Enhancing Well-Being and Alleviating Depressive Symptoms with Positive Psychology Interventions: A Practice-Friendly Meta-Analysis." *Journal of Clinical Psychology* 65: 467–87.

Spoormaker, V. I., and P. Montgomery. 2008. "Disturbed Sleep in Posttraumatic Stress Disorder: Secondary Symptom or Core Feature?" *Sleep Medicine Review* 12:169–84.

Strachan, M., D. F. Gros, K. J. Ruggiero, C. W. Lejuez, and R. Acierno. 2012. "An Integrated Approach to Delivering Exposure-Based Treatment for Symptoms of PTSD and Depression in OIF/OEF Veterans: Preliminary Findings." *Behavior Therapy* 43: 560–9.

Tull, M. T., K. S. Hahn, S. D. Evans, K. Salters-Pedneault, and K. L. Gratz. 2011. "Examining the Role of Emotional Avoidance in the Relationship Between Posttraumatic Stress Disorder Symptom Severity and Worry." *Cognitive Behaviour Therapy* 40: 5–14.

Tull, M. T., N. H. Weiss, and M. J. McDermott. (2016). "Posttraumatic Stress Disorder and Impulsive and Risky Behavior: Overview and Discussion of Potential Mechanisms." In *Comprehensive Guide to Post-Traumatic Stress Disorder*, edited by C. R. Martin, V. R. Preedy, and V. B. Patel. New York: Springer.

Wald, J., and S. Taylor. 2007. "Efficacy of Interoceptive Exposure Therapy Combined with Trauma-Related Exposure Therapy for Posttraumatic Stress Disorder: A Pilot Study." *Journal of Anxiety Disorders* 21: 1050–60.

Wald, J., S. Taylor, L. R. Chiri, and C. Sica. 2010. "Posttraumatic Stress Disorder and Chronic Pain Arising from Motor Vehicle Accidents: Efficacy of Interoceptive Exposure Plus Trauma-Related Exposure Therapy." *Cognitive Behaviour Therapy* 39: 104–13.

Weiss, N. H., M. T. Tull, A. G. Viana, M. D. Anestis, and K. L. Gratz. 2012. Impulsive Behaviors as an Emotion Regulation Strategy: Examining Associations Between PTSD, Emotion Dysregulation, and Impulsive Behaviors Among Substance Dependent Inpatients." *Journal of Anxiety Disorders* 26: 453–8.

Westphal, M., M. Olfson, M. J. Gameroff, P. Wickramaratne, D. J. Pilowsky, R. Neugebauer, R. Lantigua, S. Shea, and Y. Neria. 2011. "Functional Impairment in Adults with Past Posttraumatic Stress Disorder: Findings from Primary Care." *Depression and Anxiety* 28: 686–95.

Witkiewitz, K., G. A. Marlatt, and D. Walker. 2005. "Mindfulness-Based Relapse Prevention for Alcohol and Substance Use Disorders." *Journal of Cognitive Psychotherapy* 19: 211–28.

Zlotnick, C., C. L. Franklin, and M. Zimmerman. 2002. "Does 'Subthreshold' Posttraumatic Stress Disorder Have Any Clinical Relevance?" *Comprehensive Psychiatry* 43: 413–9.

Matthew T. Tull, PhD, is professor in the department of psychology at the University of Toledo, OH. Tull is director of the Personality and Emotion Research and Treatment laboratory, where he conducts research on the role of emotion dysregulation in the development and maintenance of post-traumatic stress disorder (PTSD), as well as the unhealthy behaviors that are often observed in PTSD, such as substance abuse, risky behaviors, and suicidal and non-suicidal self-injury. Tull has authored over 135 peer-reviewed articles, and has been the recipient of grant funding from the National Institute on Drug Abuse. In recognition of his research and contributions to the field, Tull was awarded the 2009 Chaim and Bela Danieli Young Professional Award from the International Society for Traumatic Stress Studies, and the 2010 President's New Researcher Award from the Association for Behavioral and Cognitive Therapies.

Kim L. Gratz, PhD, is professor and chair of the department of psychology at the University of Toledo, OH. Gratz directs the Personality and Emotion Research and Treatment laboratory, in which she conducts laboratory and treatment outcome research focused on the role of emotion dysregulation in the pathogenesis and treatment of borderline personality disorder (BPD), self-injury, and other risky behaviors. Gratz has received multiple awards for her research on personality disorders, including the Young Investigator's Award from the National Education Alliance for Borderline Personality Disorder (NEA-BPD) in 2005, and the Mid-Career Investigator Award from the North American Society for the Study of Personality Disorders in 2015. She has been continuously funded since 2003 (with continuous federal funding as principal investigator since 2008), and has authored more than 145 peer-reviewed publications and six books on BPD, self-injury, and dialectical behavior therapy (DBT).

Alexander L. Chapman, PhD, RPsych, is professor and coordinator of the clinical science area in the psychology department at Simon Fraser University, BC, Canada, as well as a registered psychologist and president of the DBT Centre of Vancouver. Chapman directs the Personality and Emotion Research and Treatment laboratory, where he studies the role of emotion regulation in borderline personality disorder (BPD), self-harm, impulsivity, as well as other related issues. His research is currently funded by major grants from the Canadian Institutes of Health Research. Chapman has received the Young Investigator's Award from the National Education Alliance for Borderline Personality Disorder, the Canadian Psychological Association's Scientist Practitioner Early Career Award, and a Career Investigator award from the Michael Smith Foundation for Health Research. He has coauthored ten books, three of which received the 2012 Association for Behavioral and Cognitive Therapies' Self-Help Book Seal of Merit Award. Board-certified in cognitive behavioral therapy(CBT) (Canadian Association for Cognitive and Behavioral Therapies) and dialectical behavior therapy (DBT) (DBT®-Linehan Board of Certification), Chapman cofounded a large psychology practice, and regularly gives workshops and presentations to clinicians and community groups both nationally and internationally. He also has been practicing martial arts, Zen, and mindfulness meditation for many years, and enjoys cooking, hiking, skiing, and spending time with his wife and sons.

MORE BOOKS *from*
NEW HARBINGER PUBLICATIONS

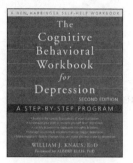
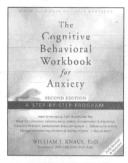

ARE YOU SEEKING A CBT THERAPIST?

The Association for Behavioral & Cognitive Therapies (ABCT) Find-a-Therapist service offers a list of therapists schooled in CBT techniques. Therapists listed are licensed professionals who have met the membership requirements of ABCT & who have chosen to appear in the directory.

Please visit www.abct.org & click on *Find a Therapist*.

Register your **new harbinger** titles for additional benefits!

When you register your **new harbinger** title—purchased in any format, from any source—you get access to benefits like the following:

- Downloadable accessories like printable worksheets and extra content

- Instructional videos and audio files

- Information about updates, corrections, and new editions

Not every title has accessories, but we're adding new material all the time.

Access free accessories in 3 easy steps:

1. Sign in at NewHarbinger.com (or **register** to create an account).

2. Click on **register a book**. Search for your title and click the **register** button when it appears.

3. Click on the **book cover or title** to go to its details page. Click on **accessories** to view and access files.

That's all there is to it!

If you need help, visit:

NewHarbinger.com/accessories

new harbinger
CELEBRATING
40 YEARS